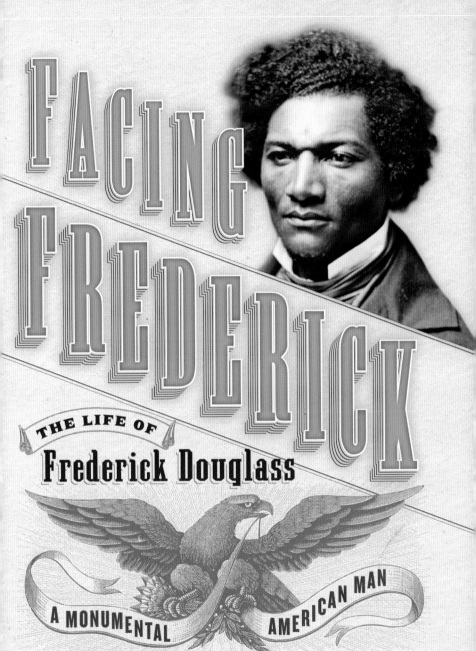

FACING FREDERICK

THE LIFE OF
Frederick Douglass

A MONUMENTAL AMERICAN MAN

TONYA BOLDEN

ABRAMS BOOKS FOR YOUNG READERS ✶ NEW YORK

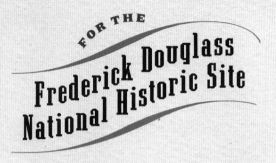

FOR THE
Frederick Douglass
National Historic Site

Cataloging-in-Publication Data has been applied for
and may be obtained from the Library of Congress.

ISBN 978-1-4197-2546-3

Grateful acknowledgment is made to the following for permission
to reprint previously published material: On page 174, "Frederick
Douglass," copyright © 1966 by Robert Hayden, from *Collected Poems
of Robert Hayden* by Robert Hayden, edited by Frederick Glaysher.
Used by permission of Liveright Publishing Corporation.

The design elements used throughout this book are sampled from original
printed material created during Frederick Douglass's lifetime (1818–1895).
The typefaces in this book are taken from or inspired by that time period as well.
They include Grecian Expanded, which was introduced in 1846 and revived by
Jordan Davies; Obsidian, which evokes the engraved typography of the 1800s
and was designed by Jonathan Hoefler and Andy Clymer; and Surveyor, which
recalls the engraved type on old maps and was designed by Tobias Frere-Jones.

Printed and bound in China
2 4 6 8 10 9 7 5 3 1

ABRAMS The Art of Books
195 Broadway, New York, NY 10007
abramsbooks.com

FREDERICK DOUGLASS

was in love with photography. . . .
He frequented photographers' studios
and sat for his portrait whenever he
could. As a result of his passion, he
also became the most photographed
American of the nineteenth century.

—**JOHN STAUFFER** et al.,
Picturing Frederick Douglass

Frederick facing right
from c. 1858 daguerreotype.

Contents

A NOTE ON
Early Photography

FREDERICK DOUGLASS, A MASTER AT managing his image, loved photography for the same reason scores of other people in the nineteenth century did: it was democratizing. Photography allowed those who couldn't afford to have their portraits painted to have images of themselves. Frederick also believed that photographs satisfied "a deep-seated want" in people—namely, to "see themselves as others see them, and as they will be seen by those [who] shall come after them."

Frederick called Louis Daguerre, one of the fathers of photography, "the great discoverer of modern times." Daguerre's process, perfected in 1839, about a year after Frederick escaped slavery, involved polishing a silver-plated copper sheet to a mirror shine, then treating that sheet with mercury vapor that rendered a light-sensitive surface onto which an image was directly exposed. The end result, a **daguerreotype** (da·guerre·o·type), was a one-of-a-kind image with incredibly sharp details. Because it is fragile (and silver is prone to tarnish), a daguerreotype was sealed under glass and placed in a protective case. So was the **ambrotype** (am·bro·-type, from a Greek word for "immortal") introduced in early 1850s. Producing an ambrotype involved exposing images onto thin sheets of glass.

Often cased but not so fragile was the **tintype**, an image printed on blackened iron. The tintype was developed in the mid-1850s, as was the **carte de visite** (or cdv or calling card). This 2½-by-4-inch photograph was produced by placing a negative onto a paper coated with an **albumen** (al·bu·men, or egg white) and salt emulsion. The image was affixed to card stock. The **cabinet card** (usually an albumen print) was mounted on larger card stock, generally 6¼ by 4¼ inches.

In *Facing Frederick*, as you learn of a legend's life, you will encounter more than a dozen photographs of the man who so loved photography and who was photographed many, many times. These photographs (with specifics provided in captions) include one taken when Douglass was in his early twenties and one taken not long before he died at the age of seventy-seven.

CHAPTER 1

A Soul to Aspire

FREDERICK FACED A DILEMMA IN mid-1846. He could sit tight and not rock the boat, or he could captain his own ship.

Nearly eight years had passed since he'd made his great escape. Nearly five since he'd begun his rise from obscure laborer to renowned warrior for the "sacred cause."

But what if his new venture failed despite his fame? A blow, yes, but would it defeat someone who had triumphed over slavery as he had? And after that, Frederick's early days of freedom

The earliest known photograph of Frederick (daguerreotype, c. 1841).

in the whaling town of New Bedford, Massachusetts, had not been easy.

One day sawing wood, another digging a cellar. Now driving a carriage or shoveling coal. Now being a chimney sweep or hoisting casks of whale oil down at the docks. Odd job after odd job, with him scrimping to keep food on the table along with a place to call home, at the start two small rooms on Elm Street facing Buzzards Bay.

Detail from *South-Eastern View of New Bedford, Mass.* (c. 1839). When this hand-colored engraving appeared, Frederick, a Southerner, was probably still adjusting to New England culture.

A few months after he settled in New Bedford, the *Liberator* came into Frederick's life. He scrimped even more to afford a yearly subscription ($2.50) to this leading antislavery newspaper. The four-page weekly became "my meat and my drink. My soul was set all on fire. Its sympathy for my brethren in bonds—its scathing denunciations of slaveholders—its faithful exposures of slavery . . . sent a thrill of joy through my soul, such as I had never felt before!"

Soul on fire, Frederick frequented local antislavery meetings. Early on just a listener, then gradually speaking up, orating. Growing bolder and more engaged, he went to meetings in other towns. The life-changing trip came on Tuesday, August 10, 1841, when he boarded the paddle-wheel steamer *Telegraph* bound for nearby Nantucket, site of a Massachusetts Anti-Slavery Society (MASS) convention.

Frederick wasn't the only black person at the three-day event held in Nantucket's library, the elegant Athenaeum. His friend Jeremiah B. Sanderson, a barber, and more than a dozen other New Bedford blacks made the journey. Residents of the island's black section of town also turned out to listen to an array of speakers. One was flinty William Lloyd Garrison, editor of the *Liberator*, Frederick's meat and drink. Garrison, like a god

William Lloyd Garrison (daguerreotype, c. 1850). Garrison—apprenticed at age fourteen to the editor of his hometown paper, the *Newburyport Herald*—was in his mid-twenties when he launched the *Liberator* in January 1831. In January 1832 he cofounded the Massachusetts Anti-Slavery Society (originally the New England Anti-Slavery Society).

to Frederick, was a MASS founder and its driving force.

When Frederick boarded the *Telegraph* he had no plans for any speechmaking. After J. B. Sanderson addressed the crowd on day two, Frederick still remained an observer. But then that evening a white man who had heard him speak in New Bedford urged him to say a few words.

As Frederick faced the overwhelmingly white crowd of five hundred, his tongue was tied; there were shackles on his mind. "I felt myself a slave." In a speech lost to history, he ultimately stopped stammering, trembling, found his voice, his way, his roar. With his entrancing baritone voice, he soared.

When Frederick finished, William Lloyd Garrison sprang to his feet and led the crowd in an impromptu call-and-response.

GARRISON: "Have we been listening to a thing, a piece of property, or to a man?"

THE CROWD: "A man! A man!"

GARRISON: "And should such a man be held a slave in a republican and Christian land?"

THE CROWD: "No, no! Never, never!"

GARRISON: "Shall such a man ever be sent back to slavery from the soil of old Massachusetts?"

In his book *Acts of the Anti-Slavery Apostles*, white minister Parker Pillsbury said this is what happened next: "Almost the whole assembly sprang with one accord to their feet and the walls and the roof of the Athenaeum seemed to shudder with the 'No, no!'"

Frederick spoke again the next day, and before the convention was over, MASS invited him to join its roster of lecturers. What's more, with MASS's help, he soon moved into a cottage of his own in the small town of Lynn. This future shoe capital of the world was about ten miles north of downtown Boston, where the *Liberator* and MASS were headquartered at 25 Cornhill Street.

A roll of thunder, a holy wonder, lionlike Frederick became MASS's most in-demand black speaker. In his mission to win souls to the sacred cause of ending slavery and to rouse converts to higher heights of activism, he delivered over a hundred speeches a year.

New England was his main stomping ground, but Frederick also spoke in New York and Pennsylvania, and as far west as Indiana. Sometimes he journeyed solo—by train, by stagecoach, on horseback. At other times with Garrison, Boston aristocrat Wendell Phillips, and other white abolitionists, as well as black ones, such as the freeborn Salem dandy Charles Remond, a barber by trade. For a time Frederick was MASS's only black speaker born enslaved.

This is an extraordinary man. He was cut out for a hero.

—**N. P. ROGERS**, a white abolitionist and newspaperman in Concord, New Hampshire

When addressing a crowd of twenty, fifty, hundreds, in a barn or church, town hall or tavern—and often without notes—Frederick captivated audiences with accounts of cruelties suffered and seen. He tore to shreds Southern propaganda that enslaved people were content and well cared for. He stressed that slavery degraded both the enslaved and the enslaver. He denounced churches that failed to support the sacred cause and damned those with slaveholders in their pulpits and pews. The idea of a Christian slaveholder was ludicrous, argued Frederick, who was by no means irreligious. He became a Christian as an

Detail from *Charles Lenox Remond* (daguerreotype, c. 1851). Remond, MASS's first black lecturer, was the son of successful entrepreneurs (barbering, hairdressing, catering). Remond, who was about eight years older than Frederick, no doubt had much to teach him when the two began lecturing together.

adolescent; as a man, a lay preacher at New Bedford's African Methodist Episcopal (AME) Zion church. And this preacher man spoke just as eloquently, just as forcefully, on the undue burdens borne by free blacks in the North as he did on slavery.

By and large blacks in the North were limited to the lowest-paying jobs. The right to serve on a jury, the right to sue over being wronged—generally none of that was allowed. At a time when only men had the right to vote, usually the only black men who had it, too, were those who owned a certain amount of property. What's more, free blacks frequently had to contend with physical assaults from whites—even children making their way to school—for some perceived slight. Or simply because they were black.

He was more than six feet in height, and his majestic form, as he rose to speak, straight as an arrow, muscular, yet lithe and graceful, his flashing eye, and more than all, his voice, that rivaled [statesman Daniel] Webster's in its richness, and in the depth and sonorousness of its cadences, made up such an ideal of an orator as the listeners never forgot.

—DAVID NEWHALL JOHNSON,
a white resident of Lynn

To a crowd in Plymouth, Massachusetts, Frederick charged that for the most part white Northerners could only tolerate blacks *"in their proper place!"* (underfoot). Such people "will not allow that we have a head to think, and a heart to feel, and a soul to aspire. They treat us not as men, but as dogs . . . and expect us to run and do their bidding." Racism put blacks in a double bind. "You degrade us, and then ask why we are degraded— you shut our mouths, and then ask why we don't speak—you close your colleges and seminaries against us, and then ask why we don't know more."

"Twin-monsters of darkness"—that's what Frederick called slavery and racism. And when it came to racism, as with slavery, he spoke from experience.

Early on in New Bedford (population about 3,000), Frederick had worked odd jobs instead of plying his trade as a caulker at a shipyard, because white caulkers threatened to quit if he was hired. So instead of earning two dollars a day, he earned about one. (Thankfully, he eventually found steady work at a candleworks and oil refinery, then at a brass foundry, where he often nailed a newspaper to a post near his bellows so that he could read as he worked.)

Later, while he was out lecturing, time and again train conductors ordered Frederick into the car for black people (usually the freight car). He sometimes resisted but then relented. More than once, when he stood his ground, he was roughed up and thrown off the train.

For a trip to Pittsfield, New Hampshire, Frederick was

denied a seat inside the stagecoach and forced to ride on its roof with the driver. During the break between lectures in Pittsfield's church, he sat on a gravestone in its cemetery for a while. Alone. In the rain. With nothing to eat, while others lunched in their homes or at the tavern, which had turned Frederick away. (Ironically, it was proslavery politician Moses Norris Jr., not an abolitionist, who welcomed him into his house.)

In Pendleton, Indiana, in the summer of 1843, the racism was near deadly. Ruffians attacked Frederick and two white colleagues as he addressed a crowd on a platform in the woods.

Big sticks and stones. Fists and feet. Frederick defended himself as best he could but was knocked unconscious and left with a broken right hand. Because the bones were not set properly, that hand plagued him for the rest of his life. After Pendleton, it was no easy thing for Frederick to write.

But write he must! He was tired of talk that he was a fake. Though he was known to show audiences his whip-scarred back, some people doubted that he had been enslaved.

Someone so dignified?

Someone so well-spoken?

A fugitive slave? How could that be?

Frederick hoped his autobiography would put an end to all that. In the winter of 1844 he picked up his pen.

Frederick's writing wasn't flawless. When he put pen to paper, "immediately" sometimes came out as "emmeadiately," "enemies" as "eneimeis" and "wrote" as "worte." Any one of his colleagues could edit his prose, but only he could tell his story. And after several years on the lecture circuit, Frederick knew how to hold people's attention.

The book began simply, straightforward: "I was born in Tuckahoe, near Hillsborough, and about twelve miles from Easton, in Talbot County, Maryland." The narrative moved on to reveal a life that was tangled, tortured.

Frederick wrote of seeing his mother only a few times. Shortly after he was born, she was sent to work on a farm twelve miles away; then she died when he was about eight.

Frederick wrote of never knowing which white man was his father and of knowing nothing about the circumstances under which he was conceived.

Frederick wrote of having at one point a closet floor for a bed.

He wrote of days of howling hunger, of feet cracked from the cold, of facing down suicidal thoughts with "the hope of being free." And there were summer Sundays spent standing on the banks of Chesapeake Bay, "with saddened heart and tearful eye," yearning to be free as he watched ship after ship move "off to the mighty ocean."

More than once young Frederick saw his aunt Hester whipped upon her naked back until her blood pooled on the floor. Later he faced physical and psychological abuse from Edward Covey, wheat farmer and notorious slave breaker. At Covey's place, sixteen-year-old Frederick worked in the fields—binding blades of grain, hauling them to the fan for winnowing—sometimes sunup to past dark, sometimes under an August sun's relentless rays, sometimes to the point of passing out. And there were beatings meant to crush his spirit, reduce him to a brute, but never succeeding. At least not for long. And never after the day he fought Covey back and beat him badly, so badly the man never again laid a hand on him.

Frederick wrote, too, of his 1836 New Year's resolution, shortly before he turned eighteen: to get free! With a handful of friends he devised a plan, but then the authorities found out about it and he landed in jail, gripped by fear of being sold into a Deep South state like Georgia, where slavery was generally more brutal, where he knew not a soul.

With pathos and passion Frederick wrote of being treated like a thing, passed around on a white person's wish or whim or because of a change in the wind.

Now, from babyhood, living with his grandparents on a farm in Tuckahoe.

Now, at age six, taken twelve miles away to the Wye House plantation in Easton to run errands, sweep yards, do other domestic work—seeing some siblings for the first time.

Now, at age eight, taken more than fifty miles away up Chesapeake Bay to Baltimore to be playmate/plaything to a ship's carpenter's son and, when older, to do menial work at a shipyard.

Nearly eight years later, back across the bay and some eighty miles away to St. Michaels.

Hired out to cruel Covey for a year.

Hired out to another farmer for a year.

Then back to Baltimore and handed over to a shipbuilder in Fell's Point to learn to be a caulker, an apprenticeship that had him at the "beck and call" of some seventy-five men.

Eighteen-year-old Frederick couldn't even learn a trade in peace. A gang of white apprentices jumped him one day. With handspikes. With sticks and stones. With carpenters shouting, "Kill him! Kill him!" And he almost lost an eye.

Frederick faced abuse after abuse for twenty long years.

A long with grim, gory, and gruesome things witnessed and endured, Frederick wrote of rare delights.

His Baltimore mistress teaching him his ABCs—until her husband, Master Hugh Auld, put a stop to that.

His getting white pals on that city's Philpot Street to continue where mistress left off.

Glorious, too, was the day when, around age thirteen, he finally had fifty cents (from

Captain Thomas Auld (unknown medium, c. 1870). Thomas Auld— brother of Hugh Auld—inherited Frederick after his wife, Lucretia, died. She had inherited Frederick after the death of her father, Captain Aaron Anthony, Frederick's owner at birth. From boyhood Frederick believed that Anthony was his father.

shining shoes on the sly) to buy a used copy of *The Columbian Orator*, a manual on the art of public speaking and a rhapsody to liberty and justice.

"On the Starry Heavens" . . . "The Dignity of Human Nature" . . . "Dialogue between a Master and Slave." The gifted, enterprising boy feasted on this three-hundred-page book's more than eighty speeches, dialogues, and essays in his quest for a finer mind, for better reading skills—skills he later passed on in clandestine schools for friends doing their best to bear up under bondage like him.

Though not in great detail, Frederick recounted his escape from Baltimore on September 3, 1838. How did he feel when he reached free soil? Like an "unarmed mariner" saved from a pirate's pursuit by a "friendly man-of-war."

Reader. Teacher. Self-emancipator. Orator. Twenty-seven-year-old Frederick added author to his accomplishments in the spring of 1845. His autobiography, *Narrative of the Life of Frederick Douglass, an American Slave*, was finished!

And it met with thunderous applause.

CHAPTER 2

One the World Over

MASS PUBLISHED *NARRATIVE*, and the *Liberator* gave it fabulous fanfare.

On Friday, May 9, 1845, the newspaper reported that the book would soon be out. It also announced that Frederick's book opened with a preface by William Lloyd Garrison, followed by a tribute from Wendell Phillips. The *Liberator* then ran Garrison's roughly 3,300-word preface. Like Phillips' letter, it vouched for the book's authenticity.

Daguerreotype, c. August 1, 1843: Frederick will continue to appear clean-shaven in photographs until the early 1850s.

Two weeks later the *Liberator* announced that Frederick's *Narrative* was available at 25 Cornhill for fifty cents a copy. The paper also ran an excerpt from the book, something it would do again and again.

Advertised in newspapers as far west as Wisconsin Territory, Frederick's 125-page book sold about 4,500 copies within three months. It was the most riveting and therefore bestselling of the roughly two dozen slave narratives published in the United States up to that point. Frederick was even more famous now.

With increased fame, Frederick faced increased danger. Like other blacks, he had lived in fear of being kidnapped and sold into slavery. There was always the possibility of his last owner getting a lead on his whereabouts and sending slave catchers after him. That's why he used aliases: first Frederick Stanley, then Frederick Johnson, and finally Frederick Douglass.

In his lectures, Frederick said little about the who and

> I hope we shall some way or other get a few copies of *Frederick Douglass' Narrative*. Your extracts from it are most interesting.
>
> —to Garrison from **JAMES HAUGHTON**, a white reformer in Dublin, Ireland

It is the most thrilling work which the American press ever issued—*and the most important.* If it does not open the eyes of this people, they must be petrified into eternal sleep. . . . It will leave a mark upon this age which the busy finger of time will deepen at every touch.

—LYNN PIONEER

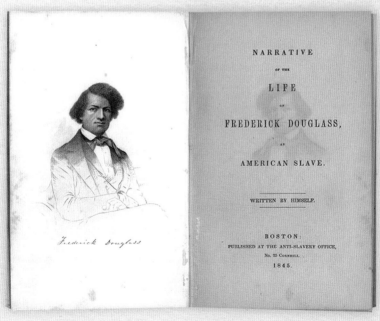

Frontispiece and title page from Frederick's *Narrative*. The original title page did not bear an engraving; it is not known how the frontispiece image was transferred onto it.

I have wept over the pages of Dickens' *Oliver Twist* . . . but Douglass' history of the wrongs [done to] the American Slave brought, not tears. . . . I groaned in the agony of my spirit and said, "Oh, Lord!, how long shall these things be?". . . I have many times heard the author vividly portray the evils of slavery. . . . But, oh!, never before have I been brought so completely in sympathy with the slave.

—to Garrison from **A WOMAN IN ALBANY**, New York, who signed her letter "A.M." With it she sent five dollars for Frederick.

where of his captivity. But in *Narrative* he revealed where he was born. He gave the names of his different owners and other taskmasters. And his real name, too. So it was now public knowledge that the abolitionist Frederick Douglass was originally Frederick Bailey. And he had been so bold as to send a copy of *Narrative* to Thomas Auld, the person who still legally owned him. The upshot was that Frederick, the fugitive, would not be hard to find. It was no secret that he lived in Lynn. Also, his lectures were advertised.

To keep his liberty, in August 1845 Frederick took flight to the British Isles, to lecture and raise funds for

MASS. Into his steamer trunk went three-piece suits, toiletries, and other necessaries for the journey, along with copies of *Narrative* to sell at his talks. He also packed slaveholders' tools of torture, including a whip and chains.

Frederick received the royal treatment in the British Isles, where he visited scores of cities in Ireland, Scotland, and England (and at least one, Wrexham, in Wales), delivering speech after speech after

> **Frederick Douglass, the Fugitive Slave, whose narrative has been so extensively read, was among the passengers that left Boston on Saturday, in the *Cambria*. He will spend several months in Great Britain, where he will no doubt be something of a "lion."**
>
> —WORCESTER'S MASSACHUSETTS SPY

speech. When he left the States aboard the steamship *Cambria,* he thought he'd be away for a few months at most, but his stay lasted much longer. This man cut out for a hero was also cut out for traveling. He toured the British Isles for nearly two years.

During his more than six hundred days across the Atlantic, Frederick never sat on a gravestone in the rain while others comfortably lunched. He lodged in the homes of leading

The Anti-Slavery Society Convention, 1840 (oil on canvas, 1841). About four hundred delegates were in London for this June 12–23 event to promote the abolition of slavery the world over. Charles Lenox Remond and Wendell Phillips were among the American delegates. The white man addressing the crowd is England's Thomas Clarkson, who spent most of his adult life fighting for the end of the Atlantic slave trade (achieved in law, if not in practice, in 1808) and for the end of slavery. The black man seated in the foreground is Henry Beckford, a Jamaican schoolteacher who spent more than twenty years in slavery. Had Frederick been an active abolitionist in 1840, he might have attended this convention, which, sadly, allowed female abolitionists only to observe.

citizens, in fine hotels. Letters to Garrison, which he rightly assumed would be reprinted in the *Liberator*, recounted examples of the first-class treatment he received, such as the breakfast for him in Cork, Ireland, in the fall of 1845. The venue, Lloyd's, was one of the city's finest hotels. Distinguished guests included Cork's mayor, Richard Dowden Richard.

We are highly gratified to find that another antislavery meeting will be held in the Independent Chapel, on this (Monday) evening [October 27, 1845]. We are glad that the people will have another opportunity of listening to a man—who is as amiable and interesting in private and social life, as he is original and eloquent in his capacity of public lecturer. —*CORK EXAMINER*, Ireland

Rarely facing racism, Frederick was reborn. He felt so free. To chat with relatives of the Scottish poet Robert Burns when in Ayr. To marvel at Edinburgh's monument to the wondrous writer Sir Walter Scott. To visit London's art galleries, botanic gardens, and other attractions. Thanks to Garrison's good friend the English orator George Thompson, while in London

Frederick had a front-row seat to a three-hour debate in Parliament. He couldn't imagine having an opportunity like that in the U.S. Congress.

Grand, too, was the day Frederick met Daniel O'Connell, the Irish Catholics' "Liberator" or "Emancipator." For years this big, bulky, magnetic man and riveting speaker had crusaded for the repeal of England's anti–Roman Catholic laws, such as those barring Catholics from serving in Parliament. After he became a member of Parliament, O'Connell campaigned for Ireland's independence from Britain, which officially santioned only Protestantism.

Detail from *Daniel O'Connell* (oil on millboard, 1834).

Frederick admired O'Connell's devotion to his people, reveled in his fighting spirit. He was grateful to him, too.

Like George Thompson, O'Connell had been among the activists who for years crusaded for the abolition of slavery in the British Empire, which finally began in 1833. Also like Thompson, O'Connell agitated for the end of slavery in the States.

A long with the pleasant, Frederick faced worrisome, even depressing things, too. In a letter to Garrison from Montrose, Scotland, in the winter of 1846, he revealed that in Dublin he dreaded stepping foot outside his host's home because the streets were "almost literally alive with beggars ... some of them mere stumps of men, without feet, without legs, without hands, without arms—and others still more horribly deformed." The sight of filthy, ragged children fending for themselves was equally heartbreaking. When Frederick got a look at some poor people's huts—"I see much here to remind me of my former condition." Scenes of squalor and suffering, a year into a great hunger that plagued Irish peasants, brought home the idea that "the cause of humanity is one the world over. He who really and truly feels for the American slave cannot steel his heart to the woes of others; and he who thinks himself an abolitionist, yet cannot enter into the wrongs of others, has yet to find a true foundation for his anti-slavery faith."

F rederick had his own demons to deal with as well. He suffered one of his "fits of melancholy" that spring. Lucky for him, when out for a walk he spotted in a shop window a violin, an instrument he loved to play. After he bought this "old fiddle," he hurried back to his hotel room. Ten minutes into a Scottish jig his depression began to lift. "They say music is good for insane people," he wrote to a friend in Lynn. And he believed everybody was more or less insane "at times."

Events back home also had Frederick down. On May 13, 1846, the United States declared war on Mexico. The pretext was a border dispute between Mexico and Texas that had escalated into skirmishes between Mexican and American soldiers. Like other abolitionists, Frederick frowned on this war as nothing but a way for slaveholding President James Polk and his fellow slaveholders to get more land for slavery's expansion. The war was about out-and-out "robbery of Mexico," Frederick wrote to a friend in the States.

Frederick was more than a celebrity lecturer and sightseer while abroad. He was also a man of business. With his supply of *Narrative* dwindling, he oversaw the publication of a new edition shortly after he arrived in Ireland. Published in Dublin in late September 1845, it had a printing of 2,000 copies.

"Well, all my books went last night at one blow," Frederick

informed his printer (and sometime host), Richard Webb, from Belfast in early December 1845. "I want more. I want more." And more books he got, but then a few weeks later, writing from Glasgow, Scotland, Frederick asked Webb to send him

View of Edinburgh from the Ramparts of the Castle, Looking East (watercolor with gum arabic over pencil on paper, c. 1846). Far left is the towering gothic memorial to Walter Scott, whose hero in his narrative poem *Lady of the Lake* is Scottish revolutionary James Douglas. Frederick took that man's surname at the urging of a friend in New Bedford. Why he added a second "s" is unknown.

three hundred copies. By then Webb was scheduled to print another 2,000 copies of *Narrative.* "Get as good, and if you can get better paper than that used in the first edition," instructed Frederick.

With those Dublin editions of *Narrative*, Frederick didn't only earn extra money (about $750 from the first edition alone)—he also learned a little about typesetting, paper, and other facets of publishing. And while he told Garrison about his publishing venture, Frederick didn't consult with him or anyone else at MASS about the changes he made. Chief among them was the preface he penned, in which he explained the reasons for his trip: to keep clear of slave catchers, to broaden his horizons, and to lecture on the horrors of slavery.

Frederick's preface preceded Garrison's and Phillips' testimonials. By making his the first voice readers heard, Frederick was taking a giant step in his road to independence. Resentment had been building for a while.

MASS had one of its white members, James Buffum, accompany Frederick to the British Isles and keep tabs on him. Also Frederick found out that some Garrisonians worried that he was becoming spoiled by all the attention lavished on him. What's more, Frederick knew that Maria Weston Chapman, Garrison's right hand, had written to Richard Webb of her concern that for Frederick the tour was all about him and his book and not about MASS. Even more insulting, Chapman had asked Webb to be watchful when Frederick collected money intended for MASS, suggesting that either he was inept at handling money or he had sticky fingers. Or both.

Even before he left for the British Isles, Frederick was getting fed up with the paternalism and we-know-best attitude of many white Garrisonians. He had been urged repeatedly to stick to the script when lecturing—just tell his story and leave the analysis to the white speakers. "We will take care of the philosophy" was how one man put it. Frederick had also been pressed to spice his talks with plantation dialect to avoid coming across as too learned.

By the time he reached the British Isles, Frederick was sick of some white colleagues seeing him in such narrow terms. A fugitive slave who gave great speeches. Not truly as an equal, or as a man. A man who devoured books, losing himself in works of New Englanders Ralph Waldo Emerson and Henry Wadsworth Longfellow, Scotland's Robert Burns and Thomas Carlyle, England's John Milton and William Shakespeare. Frederick also relished the work of the English rebel poet Lord Byron. A passage from Byron's 1812 epic poem *Childe Harold's Pilgrimage* became a motto: "Hereditary bondsmen! Know ye not / Who would be free themselves must strike the blow?"

And there was Frederick's mind, ever searching, ever seeking. He was no longer in lockstep with every aspect of Garrison's brand of abolitionism. If, in fact, he had never fully embraced it, then he was tired of faking it.

Garrison championed Disunion: a call for the free states to break away from the slave states. "No Union with Slaveholders!" Garrison practically shouted from the rooftops, believing slaves states a corrupting influence on free states.

But if the free states jettisoned the slave states, wouldn't Frederick's 3 million brethren in bondage be essentially abandoned?

Garrison also advocated moral suasion—appeals to people's hearts and minds—as the only way to bring about an end to slavery. Never violence.

In a July 1846 letter to British reformer Elizabeth Pease penned in Belfast, Frederick—probably born of violence, subjected to violence so many times, and someone who resorted to violence himself—wrote that, no, he did not categorically repudiate all use of physical force.

Politics? Heaven forbid! said Garrison. He condemned the U.S. Constitution as a proslavery document. He called it—as he called the North-South union—a "covenant with death and an agreement with hell." The Constitution had made a deal with the devil (slaveholders), for example, with its clause allowing an enslaved person to be counted as three-fifths of a person and thereby allowing slave states not as much representation in Congress as they wanted but more than most Northerners wanted them to have. Die-hard Garrisonians contended that with slaveholders in control of the government and the government upholding slavery, the government was fundamentally evil. It was therefore immoral to vote or hold political office. Garrisonians regarded a political abolitionist—someone who sought to bring about change by working within the system— as a disgrace.

But Frederick now had a new hero in Daniel O'Connell.

William Lloyd Garrison had been imprisoned for the sacred cause, was almost lynched for the sacred cause, had bounties placed upon his head for the sacred cause, had been burned in effigy. Garrison had done so much for Frederick—been a mentor, at moments like a father—but "I was growing, and needed room."

So there Frederick was in mid-1846 wrestling with whether or not to sit tight and not rock the boat or captain his own ship. By the fall, and still abroad, he made up his mind to strike out on his own. He knew some Garrisonians would call him an ingrate. Arrogant, even. But if he didn't go his own way—how stultifying. Frederick hadn't broken free from slavery to be yoked in freedom.

And he had his freedom—his legal liberty—on December 5, 1846. Friends in Great Britain had purchased it for a little over $711 from Hugh Auld, whose brother, Thomas, had sold him the rights to Frederick back in the fall of 1845.

A few months after Frederick had his freedom, on Tuesday, March 30, 1847, there was a farewell soiree for him at the posh London Tavern. George Thompson presided over the party. Guests included English author William Howitt and Rungo Bapogee, an emissary of an East Indian prince, the raja of Satara.

Among those invited but unable to attend was the Bishop of Norwich, already scheduled to be somewhere else. So was writer Charles Dickens. When he sent his regrets, Dickens said, "I trust I need hardly say that I feel a warm interest in any occasion designed as a denunciation of slavery and a mark of sympathy with any one who has escaped from its tremendous wrongs and horrors."

At that soiree, Frederick thanked his supporters for his freedom and for all the hospitality in a nearly 13,000-word speech he called "the free upgushings of a heart overborne with grateful emotions at the remembrance of the kindness I have received in this country from the day I landed until the present moment."

That kindness included a fund-raising drive already under way to help him start a newspaper, the *North Star*, his "ship."

But before he did that, Frederick needed to spend some time with his wife and children.

CHAPTER 3

Ships upon a Stormy Sea

W HEN FREDERICK RETURNED to Lynn in late April 1847, he faced a son who was clueless as to who his father was. Two-and-a-half-year old Charley had been ten months old when Frederick went abroad.

Frederick's other two sons, Lewis and Frederick Jr., six and five, remembered him just fine. He was within fifty yards of his home when they came "running and dancing" toward him. His oldest, Rosetta, nearly eight, surely would have raced to meet her father, too, but she was at school in Albany, New York,

This c. 1850 photograph is a copy of a c. 1847 daguerreotype.

more than 150 miles due west of Lynn, where she boarded with two white family friends (and abolitionists), the sisters Abigail and Lydia Mott.

As for Frederick's wife, Anna, was she standing in the doorway beaming? How she reacted at the sight of her husband after nearly two years is a mystery. So is a lot about this woman, of whom Frederick wrote very little.

It was freeborn Anna, a laundress and housekeeper in Baltimore, who taught him to play the violin. And without her, Frederick might never have made that great escape, posing as a free sailor in a red shirt, blue trousers, black tie, and tarpaulin hat.

Anna provided the sailor's disguise and money Frederick needed for a sailor's protection pass and to take a train from Baltimore to Havre de Grace, Maryland, for a ferry across the Susquehanna River to catch a train to Wilmington, Delaware, to get a steamboat to Philadelphia, where he boarded another train. Next stop, New York City. There he spent several days homeless—and terrified—until a black man steered him to Underground Railroad stationmaster David Ruggles.

As promised, Frederick wrote to Anna from New York City. As planned, she promptly joined him. Straightaway they married. When the newlyweds left for New Bedford in mid-September on Ruggles' advice (too many slave catchers in New York City), they didn't go empty-handed. They had five dollars from Ruggles and Anna's bounty: along with clothing, she had brought dishes, cutlery, and bedding, among other needful things. Chances are Anna brought a little money with her, too. And during their early days in New Bedford, Frederick wasn't making ends meet alone. Anna, equally industrious, took in laundry and did other domestic work.

As Frederick's star rose, Anna rarely traveled with him, never craved the limelight, but stayed in the shadows. About five years older than him and not literate, Anna was apparently content to take care of hearth and home—and most important, of Frederick. When he was on the road, she sent him fresh changes of clothes. Even when she had help with the family's laundry, only she could "smooth the tucks in father's linen," remembered daughter Rosetta. "It was her pleasure to know that when he stood up before an audience that his linen was immaculate and that she had made it so." Anna also contributed to the sacred cause by participating in sewing circles in which women gathered to make toys, quilts, shawls, and other items to be sold at antislavery fairs.

23d

ANTI-SLAVERY
BAZAAR

IS NOW OPEN AT

No. 15 Winter Street,

And affords an unequalled opportunity for the purchase of articles of use and beauty, of every description.

Among them are the elegant donations of friends in FRANCE, SWITZERLAND, and GREAT BRITAIN.

A flyer for an antislavery fair in Boston (c. December 1856).

Just as Frederick never wrote of the critical role Anna played in his escape, he never told the world how she managed during his long absence and the pleasant surprise that awaited him when he returned home: a bank book showing deposits of the money he had periodically sent, along with deposits of money Anna had earned doing piecework for local shoe factories. And she did this despite being sickly.

"My dear Anna is not well," Frederick wrote an English friend upon his return. But his wife, who "seldom enjoys good health," was in better shape than he expected, well enough to go with him to Albany in a few days to see their daughter. In that same letter he hinted that he was pressing on with his plans to start his own newspaper.

For that, Frederick faced stiff opposition from many Garrisonians. They argued that he couldn't pull it off, that there was no need for another antislavery paper, and that he was most needed as a lecturer.

They also tried to dissuade him by offering him a job as a correspondent for the *National Anti-Slavery Standard*, the official weekly of MASS's parent organization, which Garrison had also helped form and of which he was president: the American Anti-Slavery Society headquartered in New York City (and for which Frederick also lectured). In a letter to Garrison, a *Standard* editor, Edmund Quincy, called Frederick cocky for asking for $2.50 per article (over the $1 Quincy thought sufficient). Quincy eventually gave in but stipulated that

Frederick couldn't earn more than a hundred dollars a year from this work.

Frederick began writing for the *Standard* while on the road. Never mind that his throat was troubling him, in early August 1847 he packed his bags and set out to tour Pennsylvania, Ohio, then New York State. During his nearly three months on the road, and once again away from his family, Frederick traveled over three thousand miles and delivered more than 150 speeches. As before, he sometimes traveled solo, sometimes with Garrison and others.

When Frederick returned to Lynn in early October, he was on course to launch the *North Star,* buoyed all the more after he went through a pile of mail. An October 1, 1847, letter from J. D. Carr, founder of a famous biscuit company in Carlisle, England,

Rochester (hand-colored engraving, c. 1850). Residents Amy and Isaac Post urged Frederick to relocate to their city upon learning that he planned to start his own newspaper.

contained a bank draft for a little over £445. This money, raised by British supporters, translated into $2,175 (equivalent to about $55,000 today). In thanking Carr a month later, Frederick told him that he had already bought "an excellent and elegant [printing] press, and nearly all the necessary printing materials."

New venture. New venue. Frederick settled on Rochester, New York, about four hundred miles west of Boston. Nicknamed the "Young Lion of the West," Rochester had begun to boom with the opening of the Erie Canal in 1825. Unlike Boston, Rochester was a hotbed of political abolitionism.

Leaving Anna and their boys in Lynn, Frederick moved to Rochester in the fall of 1847. He boarded with a black friend, Charles Joiner, a "clothes scourer" (or cleaner) who lived at 48 Atwater Street, about a fifteen-minute walk from where

[Frederick] never opened to me his lips on the subject [of the *North Star*], nor asked my advice. . . . His conduct . . . has been impulsive, inconsiderate, and highly inconsistent.

—WILLIAM LLOYD GARRISON, in Cleveland, Ohio, to his wife, Helen

Frederick rented office space in downtown Rochester.

Nothing grand. Just a single room on the second floor of 25 Buffalo Street, the Talman Building (now 25 East Main Street). White attorney Henry Hunter and D. D. T. Moore, the white publisher and proprietor of the *Genesee Farmer*, a monthly journal, were among Frederick's fellow tenants in the Talman Building, where the first issue of the *North Star* rolled off the press on December 3, 1847. Subscription price: $2 a year.

"The object of the *North Star* will be to attack Slavery in all its forms and aspects; advocate Universal Emancipation; exalt the standard of Public Morality; promote the moral and intellectual improvement of the colored people; and hasten the day of FREEDOM to the three millions of our enslaved fellow countrymen." This was the *North Star*'s mission statement.

"Right is of no sex—Truth is of no color—God is the Father of us all, and all we are Brethren." This was the initial motto of

THE NORTH STAR.

VOL. I. NO. I.   ROCHESTER, N. Y., FRIDAY, DECEMBER 3, 1847.   WHOLE NO.

From the first issue of the *North Star.*

Detail from *William Cooper Nell* (photograph of an engraving, date unknown). As a teen, this son of a middle-class couple was secretary of a Garrisonian youth group. He also worked for the *Liberator* as a messenger and printer's apprentice. In the early 1840s, he was at the forefront of Boston's equal school rights movement (achieved in 1855 and today known as the school desegregation movement). Nell wrote two of the first histories of blacks in America. The best-known one is *The Colored Patriots of the American Revolution* (1855).

the four-page weekly, which Frederick expected thousands of souls to look to for direction just as thousands escaping slavery looked to the firmament's North Star in their perilous journey to a free state.

Working with Frederick on his *North Star* was printer John Dick, a white Englishman. Serving as publisher (the person in charge of the actual production of the paper) was black Bostonian William C. Nell, another writer for the *Liberator* and MASS lecturer. Frederick also had a coeditor, someone he'd met during his August–October tour: physician Martin Delany of Pittsburgh, Pennsylvania, editor of the soon-to-be-defunct *Mystery*, the first black-owned newspaper west of the Allegheny Mountains.

That first issue of the *North Star* included a report on a

The [first issue] of the *North Star* is just what it should be–a beacon light of liberty.

—DAVID RUGGLES, Northampton, Massachusetts

recent black convention in Troy, New York, and a notice of Rochester's upcoming antislavery fair. The featured article was Frederick's nearly 3,000-word open letter to Kentucky slaveholder Senator Henry Clay. Frederick pummeled the senator for giving yet another speech pushing his pet project: colonization, getting more free blacks to leave the country, preferably for Liberia, West Africa.

In weeks to come the *North Star* offered reports on antislavery meetings, speeches by abolitionists, and notices of upcoming lectures by Frederick and other abolitionists. There was news of fugitive slaves captured and of slave catchers thwarted. There were reports on "colorphobia," as experienced in Philadelphia by David Peck, the first black graduate of an American medical school (Chicago's Rush Medical College, in spring 1847). When Dr. Peck turned up to review and possibly bid on medical books at the auction house M. Thomas & Sons, he was asked to leave because of the color of his skin.

> I hasten to congratulate you on the rising of the *North Star*.... I have read it all with entire satisfaction—much of it with delight.... I hope you will write another letter to Henry Clay, and expose his folly on the subject of colonization.
>
> —SAMUEL J. MAY, a white reformer and Unitarian minister in Syracuse, New York

The twin monsters of darkness were not Frederick's only concerns. His paper carried items on prison reform (including the abolition of the death penalty), environmental issues, the connection between dreams while sleeping and physical health, and the campaign against the consumption of alcohol, a movement known as *temperance*. There were also articles on noble souls like Dorothea Dix, who advocated for the humane treatment of the mentally ill. The *North Star* carried poetry as well.

Frederick's paper also ran letters from Martin Delany about events in his neck of the woods. After shuttering the *Mystery*, in March 1848 Delany embarked on an eight-month tour of western Pennsylvania and Ohio to lecture, gather news for the *North Star,* and, more important, raise an army of subscribers in the region. Other correspondents included James McCune Smith, a graduate of the University of Glasgow (1837) and the first black licensed physician to practice in the United States. Yet another correspondent was noted lecturer William Wells Brown, who had escaped from slavery in St. Louis, Missouri, in 1834. Two years after publishing Frederick's *Narrative*, MASS published *Narrative of William W. Brown, a Fugitive Slave*, a book almost as popular as Frederick's.

Of course, the *North Star* always carried Frederick's thoughts on current events. The uprisings against tyrannical regimes that rocked Italy, France, and other European nations beginning in January 1848: Frederick was ecstatic. During the Revolutions of 1848—also known as the Springtime of the Peoples—all Frenchmen gained the right to vote, and in Austria serfdom was abolished. Frederick longed for a storm of reform to rush onto America's shores: "We live in times which have no parallel in the history of the world," he declared. "Kingdoms, realms, empires, and republics roll to

> We regard [Frederick Douglass] as one of the most extraordinary of living men. It would seem as if Providence had raised him up to deliver his race from bondage.
>
> —*CLEVELAND TRUE DEMOCRAT*, a white-owned newspaper

and fro like ships upon a stormy sea. . . . The grand conflict of the angel Liberty with the monster Slavery has at last come. The globe shakes with the contest."

No doubt convinced that his newspaper was here to stay, in February 1848, Frederick moved his family to Rochester. In April, he purchased a two-story, nine-room brick house at 4 Alexander Street, about a twenty-minute walk from his office.

At 4 Alexander Street, chess and checkers were played; Frederick was heard singing and playing the violin (and Rosetta played the piano when school let out for the summer).

Anna cultivated a gorgeous garden at 4 Alexander Street. Gardening was one of her prime delights, probably second only to seeing to Frederick's every need and those of his guests when it came to food and drink. But not much conversation. She typically did not partake in drawing-room talk, especially if those guests were white and doubly so if they were the ones who looked down their noses at her. Instead, she would retire to the kitchen or to another part of the house.

Frederick's sanctuary was a spartan upstairs room where he kept "a list of the words he found it hard to spell," remembered former next-door neighbor Jane Marsh Parker. She was about twelve when Frederick bought the house from a white abolitionist, a sale that had many whites in the neighborhood cringing and carrying on, but, said Parker, after Frederick and his family moved in folks calmed down. "Frederick Douglass was a gentleman and a good neighbor. Mrs. Douglass chose seclusion and the children were models of behavior."

Perhaps in hopes of getting Anna to be more engaged in his public life, Frederick hired someone to teach her to read and write. It didn't work out, however. But it seems that Anna could read a little. During a sewing circle, when a young lady cross-stitched "Fredrick Douglass" onto a bookmark, Anna quickly spotted the mistake, revealing, wrote Parker, "that there was one name in the world that she could read and spell."

The move to brawny, bustling Rochester, population nearing 36,000, was hard on Anna. She had liked the much smaller Lynn, where she had a small circle of friends. Shortly after the move, in a letter to Rosetta's guardians in Albany, the Mott sisters, Frederick reported that Anna had "not been well—or very good humored since we came here."

He was soon in a bad mood, too. Several months after its launch, the *North Star* was floundering.

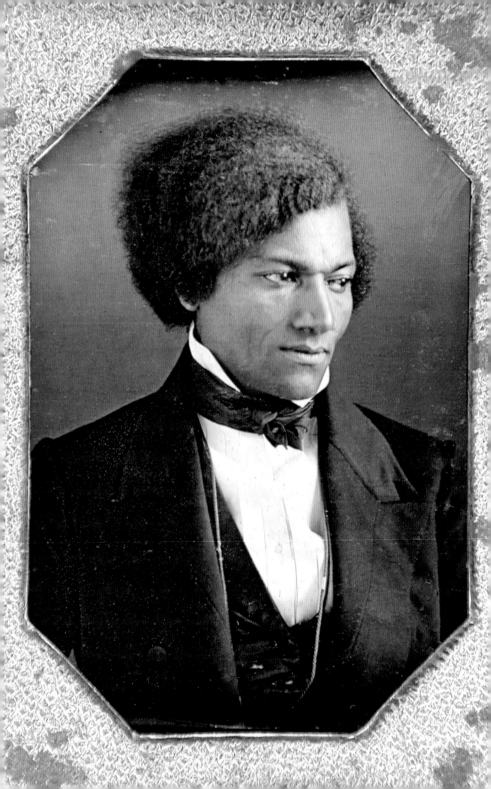

CHAPTER 4

The Voice of Inspiration

MARTIN DELANY FAILED TO raise an army of subscribers, in part because one of his little girls fell ill, then died. Other agents scattered around the North had also been unable to bring in a steady flow of subscriptions. What's more, Frederick had, as he himself admitted, "very foolishly" spent about a thousand dollars on his printing press and its paraphernalia. That

Frederick sat for this daguerreotype in May 1848 while in New York City for an American Anti-Slavery Society convention. Sometimes Frederick parted his hair on the left, sometimes on the right. Not until the mid-1850s did he settle on his iconic hairstyle evocative of a lion's mane.

"excellent and elegant" piece of machinery turned out to be a dud. After the first issue, the *North Star* was printed on another press in the Talman Building for roughly twenty dollars per issue.

"I fear I have miscalculated," Frederick wrote in the spring of 1848 to Julia Griffiths, one of his white English friends. He was referring to the support he thought his paper would get.

Whereas printing, postage, and sundries cost roughly sixty dollars a week, subscriptions brought in only about twenty-five dollars a week, and ads from bookshops, clothing stores, grocers, and the like not that much. The *North Star* had about seven hundred subscribers at a time when it needed thousands.

Though dejected, Frederick wasn't about to give up. He told Julia Griffiths he was confident that if he could keep his newspaper afloat for a year, all would be well. To that end Frederick plowed his own money into his paper—even mortgaged his home. He also took on all the speaking engagements he could get.

For striking out on his own, he had been dropped from the speakers' bureaus of both MASS and the American Anti-Slavery Society. He now secured engagements himself and with the help of other organizations, such as the Western New York

Anti-Slavery Society, formed in Rochester and with offices in the Talman Building. When Frederick wrote to Julia Griffiths, he had just returned from lecturing in upstate New York, seeking subscribers every step of the way.

In the May 5, 1848, issue of the *North Star*, Frederick appealed to the public for help. He begged people to make donations, as the paper could not yet survive on subscriptions alone. Two weeks later, "a very encouraging list" of new subscribers came in, "drops of the coming shower!"

On top of the financial strain, Frederick was having issues again with his throat, which led to a tonsillectomy on June 23. "Though I have suffered much by the operation," he told his readers a week later, he was feeling much better. He hoped to be back at the helm of the *North Star* within a few days.

When Frederick returned to work, the going was still tough. May's trickle of new subscribers did not bespeak a shower. Equally irksome: most of his subscribers were white. In the mid-July 1848 issue of the *North Star*, Frederick lashed out at the black community. Too many blacks were apathetic, he griped. He estimated that of the half million blacks in the North, "not more than two thousand can be supposed to take any special interest in measures for our own elevation; and probably not more than fifteen hundred take, read, and pay for an anti-slavery paper."

Though burdened and busy trying to save his paper, the following week Frederick journeyed down to Seneca Falls, New York, to attend a women's rights convention spearheaded by two early *North Star* subscribers, Elizabeth Cady Stanton and Lucretia Mott, sister-in-law of Abigail and Lydia Mott.

Frederick was the lone black person among some three hundred people who turned out for the historic July 19–20 convention in Wesleyan Chapel, an abolitionist church. Along with thirty-one other men and sixty-eight women, he signed the crowning achievement: the Declaration of Sentiments. Patterned after the Declaration of Independence, it demanded that women have equal pay for equal work and equality of opportunity in every walk of life—and the vote.

Women's suffrage almost didn't make it into the Declaration of Sentiments. Many women feared that asking for the vote was going too far and would open them up to great scorn. A desperate Elizabeth Cady Stanton, aware of Frederick's support for women's suffrage, pressed him to speak.

The vote, he said—"the power to choose rulers and make laws"—was "the right by which all others could be secured."

When Frederick finished, he had changed enough minds for women's suffrage to make it into the Declaration of Sentiments, though barely.

The next week the *North Star* proudly reported on Seneca Falls: "The speaking, addresses, and resolutions of this extraordinary meeting were almost wholly conducted by women ... and their whole proceedings were characterized by marked ability and dignity." Seneca Falls was not the first time people called for women's rights, but it was the first real convention for that cause, one Frederick would continue to champion. And he stayed on the move.

Two months after Seneca Falls, in early September 1848, Frederick was at another convention. This one, over which he presided, was a three-day national convention of black men held in Cleveland, Ohio. Martin Delany was among the roughly sixty delegates, along with William Howard Day, a recent graduate of Ohio's Oberlin College, and John Jones, a Chicago tailor on his way to becoming one of the wealthiest blacks in the Midwest.

Items on the agenda at that Cleveland convention included the upcoming presidential election. Delegates gave the thumbs-down to both major-party candidates: General Zachary Taylor (Whig) and Michigan senator Lewis Cass (Democrat).

Zachary Taylor, "Old Rough and Ready," who emerged from the Mexican–American War a national hero, was a slaveholder with plantations in Louisiana and Mississippi. Lewis Cass was a leading advocate for the doctrine of popular sovereignty: letting settlers decide whether to allow slavery in the nation's new territory. That new territory was the 525,000 square miles acquired from Mexico back in February 1848, through the Treaty of Guadalupe Hidalgo, which brought the Mexican–American War to an end.

Finding Taylor and Cass repugnant, Frederick and company backed the Free Soil Party candidate, former president Martin Van Buren. Founded in August 1848 in Buffalo, New York, this party (a forerunner of the Republican Party), as its name suggests, wanted slavery banned

Detail from *William Howard Day* (unknown photograph type, 1870). Born in New York City and raised in Northampton, Massachusetts, Day was the third black person to earn a bachelor's degree from Ohio's Oberlin College, an abolitionist stronghold. In 1853 he launched a newspaper in Cleveland: the *Aliened American*.

in the new territories. (Come November, Frederick's candidate wouldn't win the election. Zachary Taylor would.)

During the Cleveland convention Frederick and his comrades rededicated themselves to black liberation and elevation. They vowed to keep crusading for the abolition of slavery. They pledged to encourage and to help more blacks get an education (especially in business) and acquire skills. These men wanted to see fewer black chambermaids and chimney sweeps and more black carpenters, shop owners, lawyers, physicians, and teachers.

Keep looking up was the supreme sentiment in Frederick's keynote address. "The spirit of the age—the voice of inspiration—the deep longings of the human soul—the conflict of right with wrong— the upward tendency of the oppressed throughout the

Detail from *Portrait of John Jones* (oil on canvas, c. 1865). Jones became wealthy through his thriving tailoring business in Chicago, where he and his wife, Mary Jones, were Underground Railroad workers. This abolitionist also fought for the repeal of Illinois Black Codes, laws that curbed black civil rights (accomplished in March 1865).

world, abound with evidence complete and ample, of the final triumph of right over wrong, of freedom over slavery, and equality over caste [racism]."

Frederick asserted that no black person in the nation was free so long as any remained in chains. "We are one people," he declared. And that "we" who were free needed to strive for more independence and self-sufficiency. "To be dependent is to be degraded," he said. "Men may indeed pity us, but they cannot respect us." Then Frederick went hyperbolic.

"The houses we live in are built by white men—the clothes we wear are made by white tailors—the hats on our heads are made by white hatters, and the shoes on our feet are made by white shoe-makers, and the food that we eat is raised and cultivated by white men. Now it is impossible that we should ever be respected as a people while we are so universally and completely dependent upon white men for the necessaries of life. We must make white persons as dependent upon us as we are upon them."

Support black press! Frederick also urged. And read, read, read!—newspapers along with books to sharpen the mind and to "put to silence and to shame" white propaganda that blacks were an inferior and cursed people.

Following that invigorating convention, which garnered national coverage, Frederick returned to Rochester where he faced an outrage.

Iget along pretty well," Rosetta, now nine, began when her father inquired about school; there were tears in her eyes as she continued, "but Father, Miss Tracy does not allow me to go into the room with the other scholars because I am colored." Miss Tracy was Lucilia Tracy, principal of Seward Seminary, an exclusive all-girls school a short walk from Frederick's home. Frederick had enrolled Rosetta in Seward in protest of Rochester's segregated public schools. (For his sons he hired a private tutor.) Rosetta, whom he once called "the pulse of my heart," had started school when Frederick was out of town.

Furious over his daughter's foul treatment, Frederick demanded to speak with her classmates. Miss Tracy, an abolitionist and supposedly a Christian, agreed on the condition that if even one girl objected to Rosetta's presence, she would be expelled. After Miss Tracy learned that none of the white girls had a problem being in a classroom (or on the playground) with Rosetta, she raised the bar. Now their parents had to be polled.

The next day when Rosetta went to school, she was told to pack up her things and go home. One parent, H. G. Warner, editor of the *Rochester Courier*, had objected. Rosetta would soon be a student again in Albany, more than two hundred miles east of Rochester.

Frederick, who now added the desegregation of Rochester public schools to his list of crusades (achieved in 1857), didn't let the matter rest. He fired off a letter to H. G. Warner, chastising him for attempting to "degrade an innocent child by excluding her from the benefit of attending a respectable school." Frederick also went public. He published the letter in his newspaper, still in dire straits. But help was on the way from two very different people. One lived about 3,300 miles away as the crow flies, the other about a hundred.

I n the summer of 1849 Frederick's English friend Julia Griffiths, with her younger sister, Eliza, arrived in Rochester, ready and able to organize fund-raisers for the *North Star* and serve as its business manager. Julia Griffiths was also equipped to help Frederick become the better writer and editor that he wanted to be with tutorials on grammar and editing.

(Though he continued to send in articles, Delany ceased to be the paper's coeditor after the June 29, 1849, issue.)

Julia Griffiths' presence in Frederick's life was grist for the gossip mill. They spent long hours together at the office. They were frequently seen in the streets of Rochester, along with Eliza, strolling, arm in arm, as was the custom then (regardless of gender). What's more, the Griffiths sisters lived with Frederick and his family, which on March 22, 1849, had a new addition: another girl, Annie.

Tongues wagged even more after Eliza Griffiths married Frederick's printer, John Dick, in 1850 and the couple moved to Canada. Busybodies no doubt assumed that with Eliza out of the picture, Frederick and Julia would spend more time together. Alone. The *National Anti-Slavery Standard* would call Julia a "Jezebel." Mostly Frederick ignored the gossipmongers and focused on saving the *North Star*—and on not falling apart himself. In late 1850 thirty-two-year-old Frederick had a serious attack of what Griffiths told reformer Gerrit Smith was thought to be inflammatory rheumatism. Also, Frederick had suffered three bad falls and was "incapable of using his limbs to any extent."

The quick-tempered and combative Gerrit Smith, whom Garrison detested, was that lifesaver closer to home. After breaking with the Garrisonians in 1840, this resident of Peterboro, New York, had helped form the Liberty Party. It championed political abolitionism along with moral suasion. And this white man truly put his money—or rather his land—where his mouth was when it came to black uplift.

Detail from *Gerrit Smith* (ambrotype, c. 1840s). Smith's home in Peterboro, New York, was a station on the Underground Railroad. Frederick summed up Smith as a "great-hearted" man.

Starting in 1846, Smith, who possessed more than a half million acres, began giving blacks land in the Adirondacks: forty-acre lots, for a total of 140,000 acres to some 3,000 people by 1850. Smith, who needed to unload some of his holdings to reduce his tax burden anyway, had not only charity but also politics in mind. In New York State, only black men who owned real estate worth at least $250 could vote.

When the *North Star* made its debut, Gerrit Smith had sent Frederick a letter of congratulations and money for a two-year subscription. He later made donations. Sometimes fifty dollars, sometimes more. A friend-ship formed, cultivated through debates (by mail), chiefly about whether the U.S. Constitution was proslavery.

Between receiving Smith's letters and reading works by other thinkers, Frederick came to embrace the Constitution as an antislavery document. He saw with new eyes that its preamble stated that the document had been established to, among other things, ensure "domestic tranquility," "promote the general welfare" of its people, and "secure the blessings of liberty."

When Frederick went public with his change of mind, he faced the wrath of Garrisonians. And new horizons.

From the June 18, 1850, issue of the *North Star.* In this fancier masthead, the vignette in the center (hard to see here) is about flight to freedom guided by the North Star.

CHAPTER 5

No Time for Us to Leave the Country

THE BIG BLOWUP OCCURED IN May 1851, at the eighteenth annual meeting of American Anti-Slavery Society, held that year in Syracuse.

One subject of debate was whether the Society should endorse the *North Star* and several other antislavery papers. Garrison, among others, successfully argued that it should approve only those condemning the Constitution as proslavery.

Frederick sports chin hair in this daguerreotype taken in August 1852, in Akron, Ohio, when he went to nearby Salem, Ohio, for the Western Anti-Slavery Society's annual meeting. Other speakers included Sojourner Truth, who had escaped slavery in upstate New York in 1826. Frederick first met Truth in the early 1840s when she lived in a commune in Northampton, Massachusetts.

Frederick withdrew the *North Star* from consideration and announced that he now viewed the Constitution as antislavery. And not only that. He also now believed that abolitionists should use both moral suasion *and* political action in service to the sacred cause.

Many Garrisonians, including friend Charles Remond, howled over Frederick's shift to political abolitionism. Hostility increased several weeks later when on June 26, 1851, the *North Star,* with a circulation up to more than 4,000, was replaced by *Frederick Douglass' Paper*. "All Rights for All" its motto.

Frederick Douglass' Paper was a merger of the *North Star* and the Gerrit Smith–funded *Liberty Party Paper* published in Syracuse by John Thomas, a white man. Smith was the major financial backer of Frederick's new weekly, for which he wore two hats: publisher and editor. (*North Star* publisher William C. Nell, a Garrison loyalist, had resigned.) John Thomas was Frederick's assistant editor, and Julia Griffiths stayed on as business manager and fund-raiser (until 1855 when she returned to England, where she married Reverend Henry O. Crofts). Frederick's oldest boys, Lewis and Frederick Jr., eleven and nine, also worked on the paper, delivering and mailing it out, among other things. As always, Anna cared for the children, the home, and Frederick's linen. She also kept a tradition: a special meal on publication day.

Frederick had high hopes for his new paper and had very much wanted it to be a more handsome number. "The paper must be clean, white and strong," he had written Gerrit Smith in early June 1851. "The ink pure, black, and glossy." To get the paper off to a smart start he had asked Smith for two hundred dollars—"the rest I will raise myself."

In becoming a voter in this Union, Mr. Douglass becomes a party to the Union *as it exists*— does he not? He makes himself a partner in it, for its good and for its evil. . . . He *unites* with slaveholders and slave-traders. . . . Mr. Douglass evidently thinks he can do more good in his new position. Let him be warned of his danger. The idea of saving and enlarging his influence is a rock upon which many a reformer has suffered shipwreck.

—SAMUEL MAY JR., a white minister in Leicester, Massachusetts, and a cousin of Samuel J. May of Syracuse

> The *North Star* makes its appearance on an enlarged sheet, with new and handsome type, in excellent taste, under the title *Frederick Douglass' Paper*. We prefer the former title . . . as in this country it has a peculiar significance, in connection with slavery; because of its brevity; because it wholly avoids the appearance of egotism.
>
> —*THE LIBERATOR*

For Frederick, raising his spirits was harder than raising money at times. He still had those bouts of melancholy. In late 1851 Griffiths (no longer living at 4 Alexander Street) wrote to Gerrit Smith of her fear that Frederick was losing "his balance of mind." She said he talked of "going crazy." Also at that time, Frederick was suffering from an ulcerated throat.

Still, in the pages of his newspaper and behind lecterns, Frederick kept crusading against the twin monsters of darkness. Colonization schemes, too.

Blacks had watered America's soil with their tears, nourished it with their blood, tilled it with their hands, said

From the June 8, 1855, issue of *Frederick Douglass' Paper*, with the subtitle "Devoted to the Rights of All Mankind, Without Distinction of Color, Class, or Clime."

Frederick Douglass' Paper.

DEVOTED TO THE RIGHTS OF ALL MANKIND, WITHOUT DISTINCTION OF COLOR, CLASS, OR CLIME.

VOL. VIII.—NO. 25.　　　　ROCHESTER, N. Y., JUNE 8, 1855.　　　　WHOLE NO. 389.

FREDERICK DOUGLASS' PAPER is
Published at No. 25, Buffalo Street, (oppo-
site the Arcade,) every Friday morning, by
FREDERICK DOUGLASS.

TERMS OF SUBSCRIPTION:

Single copy, one year, ... $2 00
Three copies, " " 5 00
Five copies, " " 8 00
Ten copies, " " 15 00
Single copy, six months, ... 1 00

Voluntary Agents are entitled to retain 50
cents commission on each new yearly subscriber,
except in the case of Clubs.

Anti-Slavery.

SPEECH OF JOHN MERCER LANGSTON,
AT THE ANNIVERSARY OF THE
AMERICAN ANTI-SLAVERY SOCIETY,
Held at New York, May 9th.

Selected Matter.

SUDDEN DEATH OF A SLAVEHOLDER.

THE COMBAT THICKENS.

WHAT HAVE THEY GAINED?

THE VIRGINIA ELECTION.

REV. J. W. LOGUEN'S LETTER.

AFRICAN CUSTOMS.

SOCIAL RELATIONS—MARRIAGE.

Frederick in an 1851 debate with two white men arguing that Jamaica, West Indies, was an ideal place for free blacks to go. Yes, blacks had it hard in the States, said Frederick, but this was home. "Amid all our afflictions there is an invincible determination to stay right here."

Some blacks disagreed. The United States would never be a true home. They'd always be outcasts. White hatred was too strong, too deep. Thousands of blacks had emigrated over the years (mostly to Liberia). And interest in emigration was now on the rise, thanks to the Compromise of 1850.

Crafted by Senator Henry Clay, this series of laws sought to ease the tension between slave and free states over the land acquired through the Mexican–American War. The laws included admitting California as a free state and abolishing slave trading (but not slavery) in the District of Columbia— two things Frederick could cheer. But with them came what he called "a hell-black enactment": a new, more vicious Fugitive Slave Law. Now anyone who aided people who took their liberty could be fined up to a thousand dollars and imprisoned for up to six months. What's more, federal marshals had to assist slave catchers and could even dragoon other people into doing the same. With a black person's word carrying no weight, free blacks were in greater jeopardy of being hauled into slavery.

After Clay's compromise passed in September 1850, thousands of blacks—freeborn, freed, and self-emancipated—fled the States, most for Canada. This exodus surely led to a spike in Frederick's Underground Railroad work. He had been serving as a conductor and stationmaster since he moved to Rochester, about a hundred miles east from St. Catherines in Canada West (present-day Ontario). Anna was on duty, too. As Rosetta remembered, she was "called up at all hours of the night, cold or hot as the case may be, to prepare supper for a hungry lot of fleeing humanity."

Frederick and Anna aided about four hundred people over the years. He likened it to "an attempt to bail out the ocean with a teaspoon," but one less person in bondage was a triumph still. White coworkers included Rochester pharmacist Isaac Post and his wife, Amy—both good friends; former head of the girls' department of Canajoharie Academy Susan B. Anthony, another Rochester friend; and farmer Gideon Pitts Jr. and his wife, Jane, in Honeoye, New York, about thirty miles south of Rochester. Black conductors and stationmasters in upstate New York included Frederick's good friend Reverend Jermain

Wesley Loguen, a native of Tennessee who, like Frederick, had been sired by a white man (his owner), had escaped slavery in the 1830s when in his twenties, and would in a few years, write his autobiography.

It is believed that "fleeing humanity" was brought to Frederick's house at least once by Harriet Tubman, to whom he would one day write, "I have wrought in the day—you in the night. I have had the applause of the crowd and the satisfaction that comes of being approved by the multitude, while the most that you have done has been witnessed by a few trembling, scarred, and foot-sore bondmen and women, whom you have led out of the house of bondage, and whose heartfelt 'God bless you' has been your only reward. The midnight sky and the silent stars have been the witnesses of your devotion to freedom and of your heroism."

This risky business of helping freedom-seekers became a little less so when in 1852 Frederick moved his family from 4 Alexander Street to a secluded hillside farm near Rochester's southern city line. This new home was on the South St. Paul Road (renamed South Avenue in the mid-1850s).

As Frederick served on the Underground Railroad, as he lectured and wrote, as he got his newspaper out, he had to reach deep into a reservoir of faith to keep going. Faith in the land of his birth. Faith that more white people would come to their senses and recognize that people are of one blood. Faith, too, that God was on his side. Faith kept Frederick hoping on.

All was not grim, even his famous speech on July 5, 1852, in Rochester's Corinthian Hall, in which he essentially raised the question, "What to the slave is the Fourth of July?"; in which he said to white people, "This Fourth [of] July is *yours*, not *mine*. *You* may rejoice, *I* must mourn"; in which he said that to an enslaved person "your celebration is a sham; your boasted liberty, an unholy license; your national greatness, swelling vanity; your sounds of rejoicing are empty and heartless; your denunciations of tyrants, brass fronted impudence; your shouts of liberty and equality, hollow mockery; your prayers and hymns, your sermons and thanksgivings, with all your religious parade, and solemnity, are, to him, mere bombast, fraud, deception, impiety, and hypocrisy—a thin veil to cover up crimes which would disgrace a nation of savages"— even that speech closed on a note of hope.

Frederick concluded with a recitation of Garrison's poem "The Triumph of Freedom," a prayer for God to "speed" the year, the day, the hour "of jubilee," the day of liberty. It ends:

"And never from my chosen post, / Whate'er the peril or the cost, / Be driven."

Frederick remained the optimist after May 30, 1854, the day the Kansas-Nebraska Act cleared Congress. It repealed the Missouri Compromise of 1820, which, in admitting Maine to the Union as a free state and Missouri as a slave state, banned slavery in the rest of the land acquired in the Louisiana Purchase (1803) above the parallel 36° 30′. This land included the territories of Kansas and Nebraska. Now, said the Kansas–Nebraska Act, slavery in these lands would be a matter of popular sovereignty.

Two months after passage of the Kansas–Nebraska Act, in a commencement address at Ohio's Western Reserve College, Frederick was still keeping hope alive: "The ten thousand horrors of slavery, striking hard upon the sensitive soul, have bruised, and battered, and stung, but have not killed. The poor bondsman lifts a smiling face above the surface of a sea of agonies, *hoping on, hoping ever*." If people in bondage were not in utter despair, how could he be?

Frederick hoped on, hoped ever, while at work on his second autobiography, the more than 450-page *My Bondage and My Freedom*. New details about his youth included time spent with a Mr. Lawson, an elderly black man in Baltimore who drove a dray and lived a "life of prayer." Lawson, Frederick's spiritual father, had told the lad that God had "a great work" for him to do.

Near the end of *My Bondage*, published in August 1855 with a dedication to Gerrit Smith and an introduction by good friend Dr. James McCune Smith, Frederick said of the abolitionist movement, "I am sober, but not hopeless." His hope lay in the belief that the antislavery movement was unstoppable. If a thousand of his comrades were "struck down," its ranks would remain "invincible." In his closing line he wrote, "it is the faith of my soul that this anti-slavery cause will triumph."

Frederick hoped on, hoped ever, after May 21, 1856, when proslavery forces laid waste to Lawrence, Kansas, an antislavery stronghold.

> This morning is the third day since the publication of Frederick Douglass' ... *My Bondage and My Freedom*. We learn from the publishers that not a single copy of the first edition remains on hand. 5,000 copies comprise the edition, and in two days the whole are gone.
>
> —*AUBURN DAILY ADVERTISER*

After May 22, when on the Senate floor South Carolina slaveholder Representative Preston Brooks used his walking stick to beat nearly to death Massachusetts abolitionist Senator Charles Sumner. Payback for Sumner's insults against Southern soil and Brooks' family in a recent speech, "Crime against Kansas," a condemnation of forces working to keep that territory from being free soil.

Frederick hoped on, hoped ever, after Preston Brooks was fined $300 but received no prison time for his crime against Sumner.

Frederick's hope was not dashed after March 6, 1857, when the U.S. Supreme Court handed down its 7–2 Dred Scott decision. The Court denied Dred and Harriet Scott their freedom, freedom their attorney thought they could get because their owner had them living on free soil for quite a while (some of it in Wisconsin Territory). But, said Chief Justice Roger Taney, the Scotts had no standing in federal court as they were not—and even if free never could be—U.S. citizens. Added to that, neither the Declaration of Independence nor the Constitution gave black people rights, because they were a people "so far inferior that they had no rights which the white man was bound to respect." The ruling also said that Congress had no right to ban slavery in the territories.

"You will readily ask me how I am affected by this devilish decision—this judicial incarnation of wolfishness?" That was Frederick a month later in a nearly 8,000-word speech in Rochester. His "hopes were never brighter than now." Yes, the Supreme Court was a powerful institution, but "the Supreme Court of the Almighty is greater." Frederick believed outrage over the Dred Scott decision would result in a surge of support for the sacred cause.

But other blacks insisted that the situation was hopeless, and emigration the only recourse. New York's Reverend Henry Highland Garnet was in this camp. In 1858 Garnet formed the African Civilization Society, calling for the black community's best and brightest to join him in building a cotton industry in Africa's upper Niger River region in present-day Nigeria.

Frederick argued that Garnet's Society—like Clay's American Colonization Society—was based "upon the lying assumption that white and black people can never live in the same land on terms of equality." That upbraiding wasn't in *Frederick Douglass' Paper* but in the February 1859 *Douglass' Monthly*, launched in June 1858 as a four-page digest aimed at British readers. It became a separate sixteen-page publication in

January 1859, a month before Frederick's critique of Garnet's movement.

Back in 1849, when Garnet promoted immigration to Jamaica, Frederick tried to sabotage his upcoming lecture tour in England in service of the Free Produce movement (a boycott of food and other items created by slave labor). Frederick basically said, *England Beware!* Garnet's motives were suspect, he asserted, because the man had never promoted the Free Produce movement in the States.

Frederick also went to war with his former coeditor Martin Delany over emigration. His paper covered Delany's convention on emigration in Cleveland during the summer of 1854, but mostly in ways that belittled it. Delany was then advocating immigration to the Caribbean, Central America, or South America. A few years and two more immigration conventions later, it was Africa. In mid-1859 Delany went on an exploratory mission to Yoruba, most of which is in present-day Nigeria.

The Caribbean, Central America, South America, Africa— Frederick thought it all absurd. Black emigrationists were as wrongheaded as white colonizationists.

Fueling the friction was Delany and Garnet's unabashed pride in their skin color. Both claimed that only African "blood" flowed through their veins, thus making them pure, unadulterated. Frederick, light skinned and half white, found that kind of talk irksome. "I thank God for making me a man simply," he allegedly once scoffed, "but Delany always thanks him for making him a *black man*." For their part, Garnet and Delany thought Frederick craved friendships with white people overmuch.

> I knew, sir, that in your hot pursuit after a worthless and a transient fame, you would sometimes stoop to mean things, but I never dreamed that you would ever sink so low, that you would have to reach up, standing on tip-toe, to find that level of meanness where common knaves are inclined to pause. Ah, sir, the green-eyed monster has made you mad.
>
> —**HENRY HIGHLAND GARNET**, in a letter to Frederick upbraiding him for besmirching Garnet's character

While Frederick clamored for free blacks to stay in the States and fight for liberty and justice, he was nowhere near as zealous as his friend John Brown, who cast himself as an avenging angel in a drama penned by God. When the two men first met back in late 1847, in Springfield, Massachusetts, where

Detail from *Henry Highland Garnet* (carte de visite, c. 1871). Like Frederick, Garnet was born in Maryland (New Market). He was nine when he escaped slavery with his parents. The family settled in New York City, where his schoolmates included Frederick's good friend Dr. James McCune Smith. A graduate of the Oneida Institute in Whitesboro, New York, Garnet pastored several Presbyterian churches in the Northeast starting in 1842.

John Brown then lived, Frederick was awestruck by the "lean, strong, and sinewy" Brown, whose bluish-gray eyes were "full of light and fire" when he spoke. Brown, nearly twenty years older, arrived in Rochester in late January 1858 and stayed in Frederick's home for about a month. During that time he spent hours holed up in a bedroom working on his Provisional Constitution for the slavery-free state in the Allegheny Mountains he planned to found by force.

Phase one was a raid on the federal arsenal in Harpers Ferry, Virginia (now in West Virginia), with a band of stouthearted men. That done, they'd rally enslaved people in the area to a great rebellion. As Brown worked on his plan, he found financial backing from a group of white men known as the "Secret Six."

"Come with me," Brown pleaded with Frederick when they

met in a stone quarry near Chambersburg, Pennsylvania, in early fall of 1859. Frederick didn't think the plan wise, didn't think it would succeed. He told his friend no.

Frederick was lecturing in Philadelphia's National Hall on October 17, 1859, when someone interrupted with the news that John Brown's raid, launched the day before, had failed. His guerrilla army of twenty-two men, five of whom were black and three of whom were his sons, were no match for a detachment of Marines. Two of Brown's sons

Detail from *Martin Robison Delany* (carte de visite, c. 1863). Born free in Charles Town, Virginia (now in West Virginia), in 1833, Delany began a medical apprenticeship with Dr. Andrew McDowell in Pittsburgh, Pennsylvania, and later studied with other physicians. In the fall of 1850, along with Daniel Laing Jr. and Isaac Snowden (both of Boston), Delany became one of the first blacks admitted to Harvard Medical School. They were expelled within a few months after about a quarter of their white classmates threatened to withdraw from the school if the black men stayed.

and eight other men were dead; seven, including a wounded John Brown, captured.

And Frederick now faced the possibility of capture himself. The authorities had discovered a letter from him among

Detail from *John Brown*, by unidentified photographer (daguerreotype, 1856). The year this photograph was taken was the year this New Englander led a massacre of proslavery men who lived along Pottawatomie Creek in southern Kansas. It happened in May 1856, shortly after proslavery forces sacked Lawrence, Kansas, and Preston Brooks attacked Charles Sumner in the Senate.

Brown's belongings. It had nothing to do with the raid, but it was enough to charge Frederick as a coconspirator and issue a warrant for his arrest.

Frederick fled Philadelphia, making his way to Hoboken, New Jersey, where he stayed overnight with a friend. The morning papers had him in a panic. The government was leaving no stone unturned, as he later wrote, in "ferreting out and bringing to punishment all who were connected with the Harpers Ferry outrage, and that search would be made for papers as well as persons."

Papers and persons.

There were letters from John Brown in his locked desk drawer at home. Also a copy of Brown's Provisional Constitution. Frederick quickly got a telegram to a trusted friend in

Rochester: "Tell Lewis (my oldest son) to secure all the important papers in my high desk." Lewis did as told. As Frederick later wrote, "The mark of the chisel with which the desk was opened is still on the drawer."

Frederick didn't hide out in Hoboken for long. By a circuitous route he returned to Rochester, then headed to Canada and finally to England, arriving there on November 24. Before he left the States, he drafted a letter to his readers, which ran in the November *Douglass' Monthly*. In it, he swore he had never encouraged John Brown's raid, never promised to take part in it. He also said that he was scheduled to lecture in England long before Harpers Ferry. That was the last issue of his paper readers would see until he returned.

About a week after Frederick reached England, on December 2, 1859, John Brown, found guilty of conspiracy, treason, and murder, was led to the gallows outside a jail in Charles Town, Virginia. Said Frederick of his friend years later: "His zeal in the cause of my race was far greater than mine—it was as the burning sun to my taper light—mine was bounded by time, his stretched away to the boundless shores of eternity. I could live for the slave, but he could die for him."

After learning that John Brown would hang, the great-hearted Gerrit Smith, a member of the "Secret Six," suffered a mental breakdown and wound up in the New York State asylum in Utica, New York.

Frederick was in Glasgow, Scotland, when, in late March 1860, word of another tragedy reached him, this one a thousand times more wrenching than Brown's execution and Smith's breakdown. Frederick's younger daughter, Annie, a voracious reader and a fine writer, stricken with a brain disease, had died on March 13. She had been buried three days later, six days before her eleventh birthday.

Throwing caution to the wind, Frederick caught the first steamer he could. He reached Rochester in April, then lay low for a few weeks until the charges against him as a John Brown accomplice were dropped.

While Frederick mourned Annie, "the light and life" of his house, he was no doubt wrestling with the fact that in publishing two papers, he had bitten off more than he could chew. "We shall speak to you *weekly* when we can, and *monthly* when we must," he announced in the August

1860 *Douglass' Monthly*, which carried below the masthead a quote from the Old Testament book of Proverbs (mistakenly attributed to Ecclesiastes in early issues): "Open thy mouth for the dumb, in the cause of all such as are appointed to destruction; Open thy mouth, judge righteously, and plead the cause of the poor and needy." When he suspended *Frederick Douglass' Paper*, he thought it would be temporary and looked forward to its making a comeback, but that never happened.

In that same issue of *Douglass' Monthly* in which he announced the weekly's suspension, Frederick, now forty-two, told his readers that he was having a hard time hoping on, hoping ever. After thirty years of American abolitionism—speeches, articles, rallies, petitions—"The future of the anti-slavery cause is shrouded in doubt and gloom." Countless men and women had done their utmost to make people aware of the horrors of slavery. Yet the abomination still existed. The problem wasn't ignorance, he concluded. Not enough people gave a damn.

Yet Frederick couldn't withdraw from the field. The sacred cause was his life. So in the 1860 presidential election he backed the Republican Party's candidate, Abraham Lincoln from Illinois. Never a slaveholder, Lincoln thought

slavery wrong and vehemently opposed allowing it in the territories. He was, however, not an abolitionist—not advocating the immediate, unconditional end of slavery throughout
the land.

Still, how could Frederick not root for Lincoln, given his
opponents? Northern Democrats ran Illinois's proslavery
senator Stephen Douglas (father of the Kansas-Nebraska
Act); Southern Democrats backed the sitting vice president (under President James Buchanan), John Breckinridge
of Kentucky, a slaveholder; and the newly minted Consti-
tutional Union Party chose John Bell of Tennessee, also a
slaveholder.

The enemy of Frederick's enemy was his friend. The
slaveholding politicians who ruled the South and who supported Democrats detested Lincoln for his stance against slavery's expansion. They threatened that the slave states would
secede if he won the presidency. After he did, on November
6, 1860, these "Fire-Eaters," as they were nicknamed, were in
a frenzy.

A tantrum to wheedle more compromises out of the
North—that's what Frederick thought when South Carolina seceded on December 20, 1860. He was sickened by the

way many white Northerners wrung their hands when other states seceded. Mississippi, Florida, Alabama, Georgia, Louisiana, all in January 1861, then Texas on February 1. That was three days before a peace conference in Washington, D.C., in which politicians tried to devise ways to cobble the Union back together.

Frederick was glad the peace conference failed. The time for compromise was over. There could be no reconciliation between freedom and slavery—no peace between proslavery and antislavery people. And if there was not "wisdom and virtue enough in the land" to end slavery, "then the next best thing is to let the South go to her own place and be made to drink the wine cup of wrath and fire, which her long career of cruelty, barbarism, and blood shall call down upon her guilty head."

After March 4, 1861—Inauguration Day—Frederick concluded that there was not wisdom and virtue enough in President Lincoln. In his address from the East Portico of the Capitol, the new president stressed that he had no plans to meddle with slavery in the states where it already existed. He vowed that his administration would uphold the Fugitive Slave Law. He practically begged the breakaway states calling

DOUGLASS' MONTHLY.

"OPEN THY MOUTH FOR THE DUMB, IN THE CAUSE OF ALL SUCH AS ARE APPOINTED TO DESTRUCTION ; OPEN THY MOUTH, JUDGE RIGHTEOUSLY, AND PLEAD THE CAUSE OF THE POOR AND NEEDY."—1st Eccl. xxxi. 8, 9.

VOLUME III.
NUMBER VIII.

ROCHESTER, NEW YORK, JANUARY, 1861.

PRICE—
ONE DOLLAR PER ANNUM.

CONTENTS OF THE PRESENT NUMBER.

DOUGLASS' MONTHLY.

THE BOSTON MOB OF DECEMBER, 1860.

The details of this mob have found their way to the public through a thousand different channels, and a pretty full description of it may be read in our present monthly. Nothing need be added to what has been said in this line ; and yet, as one who witnessed the mob, and was in some sort a subject of its fury, we may properly be expected to add our testimony as to its character and merits.

In the first place, it was no vulgar, passionate outbreak of popular feeling, led on by the humble and poor, the base and the ignorant, roused to fury by what they deemed an unwarrantable and intolerable outrage.— It may well be described, as it has been—the gentlemen's mob. Its rank and file, not less than its leaders, claim position with the upper classes of Boston society. They were gentlemen of the ' DOLLAR STAMP,' well dressed, well conditioned, well looking, and doubtless, on occasions, pass very well for gentlemen.— We have no disposition to underrate their quality. One could see at a glance that these gentlemen were none of your practiced ruffians, and were badly fitted to play the ruffian's part. Their leader, Mr. RICHARD S. FAY, though he had been fully informed of the part he was to play as Chairman of the captured meeting, and had his resolutions all ready to offer, and his little speech already prepared, evinced much agitation. He made a strong effort to control his nerves, and to seem composed ; but it was of no use—he trembled like a man with the palsy. A friend of ours, observing his trepidation, sang out, ' Read away ; nobody is going to hurt you !' The hit was excellent, but did but little to reassure our nervous Chairman, for he seemed to tremble all the more for the interruption. In all his movements he appeared conscious of the mean, wicked and lawless business in which he was engaged, and before he got through, evidently wished himself well out of the scrape into which he was hopelessly plunged.

It will be seen by recurring to the detailed accounts in our other columns, that the mob, though vigorously supported by the Mayor and police, was, after all, a failure. The JOHN BROWN anniversary was celebrated in Boston, and the friends of freedom and free speech had their say. After the Tremont Temple meeting was broken up by the Mayor and the mob, Mr. J. SELLA MARTIN instantly announced that the meeting would be continued in the evening at the Joy Street Baptist Church, of which he is the pastor. The announcement was brave, but the holding of the meeting under the circumstances was more brave. It tested the mettle of the men engaged in it. Enemies threatened; friends deprecated, inflammatory appeals were circulated, the authorities were against it, and at one time it seemed that the officers of the ' Joy Street Church' would quail, and refuse the use of the house. Mr. MARTIN, upon learning that his trustees were about to shut the doors of his church against the meeting, promptly told them that if that were done, they could never open their doors to him again. Such conduct needs no commendation. The church was opened, the officers nobly deciding that it were better that the house should be pulled down than that colored people should surrender the right of free speech at the dictation of an unprincipled and lawless mob, and of cowardly officers unwilling to do their duty. We have never seen men and women more fully in earnest. Too much honor cannot be awarded to Mr. WENDELL PHILLIPS for the part he bore in the Joy Street meeting. Through a mob raging in the street, threatening to tear down his house over the head of his wife—she an invalid— with Mrs. CHAPMAN on his arm, Mr. PHILLIPS walked calmly to the meeting, and took his seat with the despised and hated, and by his surpassing eloquence thrilled and strengthened all anti-slavery hearts, while he overwhelmed all opposition. JOHN BROWN, Jr., made a characteristic speech, and in a characteristic manner. Much of the quiet of the evening was due to his words and presence. He made no secret of being in a state of complete preparation for any violence that might be offered. Every body saw that Mr. BROWN meant just what he said, and seemed to feel that he would translate his words into deeds at the first moment that circumstances might make it necessary to do so. But we did not take up the subject for details, nor for eulogies of the good men who acted a noble part in opposition to the mob.

The chief thing is to get at its true character, and disclose its relations and bearings on the age and body of the times. It was an incident small in itself, but vast in its relations and bearings. It makes a page in the history of the great struggle between liberty and slavery. It shows less what has been accomplished, than what yet remains to be. It proves that there are men even in Boston— the seat of American learning, and the cradle of American liberty—who are ignorant of, or faithless in, the first principles of American liberty ; that they are yet in bondage to the delusion that truth can be put down by persecution ; that violence is the remedy for error of opinion ; and that sentiment can be sub- dued by force. They seem not to have learned, with the history and experience of a quarter of a century, that it has been precisely by such mobs that the anti-slavery sentiment has at last been able to break up all old political issues, bring on the 'irrepressible conflict,' overthrow the old political parties, remodel public opinion, change the current of religious influence, make slave-hunting unpopular, and make South Carolina almost mad to get out of the Union.

The contemners of freedom, and the opponents of free institutions will gather fresh strength from this new illustration of American respect for law, and the example of the fidelity of Democratic officers in the execution of law. They will find in it new proof of our barbarism, and of the fact that men are here governed by the mob rather than by known and established laws. The friends of freedom everywhere will regret and condemn this new reproach to free institutions, and see in it cause for still greater exertions to enlighten the public mind and improving the public heart with respect to the true principles of human liberty. No such demonstrations can be permanently injurious, unless the friends of freedom refuse to make the right use of the occasions which they furnish—a neglect not likely to be illustrated in Boston. Already Governor ANDREWS has made it the subject of pointed rebuke, and WENDELL PHILLIPS has denounced the mob in the presence of four thousand, in Music Hall ; and we hear that a more general and influential assertion of the sacredness of the right of speech is still to be given in the very face of the gentlemanly mob.

The actors in the disgraceful and scandalous riot must wince under the exposures to which they are being subjected, and feel mortified that they have so signally failed to convert Boston into an echo of Charleston, and to make Massachusetts an appendage of the blood-stained cotton fields of the Carolinas.— The miserable plot failed, not merely because it was badly managed, nor because its object was bad—for bad causes have their victories as well as good ones—but because the actors in it were insincere. To serve even a wicked cause successfully, requires something like honest and earnest devotion. This Boston mob lacked all honest elements. It was an imposition, a fraud, a sham, lip service, got up for show—a newspaper mob, a show case for Southern windows, a thing of trade, designed to preserve the union of Boston pockets with Southern money. This is its only significance. Though the actors in it may hate liberty, they don't love slavery. They meant to deceive the South by all abounding professions of devotion to slavery ; but the South is not green enough to accept such professions, so that the hypocrites, while well lashed at home, are despised at the South.

—A bold attempt to kidnap a colored boy was thwarted in New York last week. Nothing was done to the kidnappers.

themselves the Confederate States of America to return to the fold. There was one comfort for Frederick: He would soon get away from this weak-willed nation. A trip to Haiti was on his calendar.

Since late 1860 *Douglass' Monthly* had carried ads and articles on the Haitian Emigration Bureau, funded by the government of Haiti, the first black republic in the Western Hemisphere. Based in Boston, the bureau was run by Scottish abolitionist and journalist James Redpath, a friend of John Brown's. Redpath's lieutenants included Henry Highland Garnet and John Brown Jr. (who had not participated in his father's raid).

With hope flagging, Frederick no longer blasted every emigration scheme, and he wanted to check out Haiti for himself. He and his daughter, Rosetta, were scheduled to leave in late April 1861 for a ten-week trip, but then came a Southern storm that stopped him from packing his bags.

"This is no time for us to leave the country," Frederick told his readers.

From the January 1861 *Douglass' Monthly*. The lead article is about the attack in Boston's Tremont Temple on Frederick and other abolitionists during a commemoration of the one-year anniversary of John Brown's execution.

CHAPTER 6

We Are All Liberated

AS DAY DAWNED ON FRIDAY, APRIL 12, 1861, Confederate forces fired on Union-held Fort Sumter in Charleston, South Carolina. Shot and shell steadily besieged the fort until its commandant surrendered on the afternoon of April 13. Two days later President Lincoln declared the breakaway states to be in rank rebellion and called for 75,000 troops to crush it. Within weeks Virginia, Arkansas, Tennessee, then North Carolina joined the Confederate States of America.

A carte de visite taken on January 21, 1863, the day Frederick spoke at Michigan's Hillsdale College. He chose a full-length pose instead of his usual head-and-shoulders shot. He also opted for a prop: not surprisingly, a book.

With the outbreak of the Civil War, Frederick's hopes soared.

A war to save the Union! That's what Lincoln and most white Northerners declared.

Oh, no! said Frederick and other abolitionists, who saw things in biblical, apocalyptic terms. This was a war to end slavery—a great holy war at that, a war that would climax with a cleansing and redemption of a wayward nation. So there was no going to Haiti for Frederick. He had to stay and fight. As always, he did so with pen and tongue.

Soul on fire once again, Frederick damned Lincoln for making Union soldiers return people who escaped slavery to their owners—even when those owners were rebels. He scolded Lincoln for not declaring black captives free and for not urging them to rise up! He lashed out at Lincoln for trying to entice slave states that didn't join the Confederacy—the border states of Delaware, Kentucky, Maryland, and Missouri—to consent to compensated gradual emancipation: let the U.S. government pay slaveholders to free people in due time. In his appeals to the border states the president tried to convince them that most blacks would leave the country—something he advocated and another thing Frederick criticized him for.

Frederick also blasted Lincoln for not allowing black men to join the Union Army. "The national edifice is on fire," he raged in an editorial. "Every man who can carry a bucket of water or remove a brick is wanted; but those who have the care of the building, having a profound respect for the feeling of the national burglars who set the building on fire, are determined that the flames shall only be extinguished by [white hands].... Such is the pride, the stupid prejudice, and folly that rules the hour."

As bombs, bullets, and bayonets bloodied and blew away lives, Frederick ratcheted up his rhetoric on slaveholders. He had often called them fiends, pirates, thieves. Now he cast them as even more monstrous, as evil incarnate. In his paper Frederick passed on reports of ghoulish goings-on in the Confederate states: of

> The same cruel prejudice which excludes us from the halls of science also repels us from the militia and the standing army. Therefore to offer ourselves for military service now is to abandon self-respect and invite insult.
>
> —REVEREND ELISHA WEAVER, editor of the *Christian Recorder*, organ of the AME Church

rebels making candles "from tallow and fat fried from dead Yankees." In a speech in upstate New York on the Fourth of July, 1862, in declaring slavery and *only* slavery the cause of the war—"its root and its sap, its trunk and its branches, and the bloody fruit it bears"—he told of Confederates making "drinking vessels" out of Union soldiers' skulls and sticks for battlefield drums out of their arm bones. With tales of such atrocities, whether true or not, Frederick sought to whip up more hatred for rebels in the North and make the point that without the Union, the rebel states would become even more barbarous.

DEAR SIR: –In your last issue . . . you state that the signs of the times are favorable to the downfall of slavery. . . . Now do, in your next issue, give us some of the signs. In the last week's N.Y. Post, I see that our army on the Potomac has been in chase of a fugitive, and ran him down and sent him back to his master under an escort of soldiers. Now, if this is one of your favorable signs, I must disagree with you. . . . I am sick and disheartened.

—S. DUTTON of Meredith, New York

With the war came mended fences and buried hatchets. Frederick once again lectured with William Lloyd Garrison, Wendell Phillips, and other abolitionists who had turned against him—and who now set aside their pacifism. Like them, despite his frustration with Lincoln, Frederick kept his hopes high that the Slave Power would be vanquished.

As Frederick employed his pen and tongue perhaps more mightily than ever before, the jubilation came bit by bit.

May 24, 1861: At Virginia's Fort Monroe, Union General Benjamin Butler declared three black men who sought sanctuary at his fort "contraband of war": enemy property of military value and so legal to keep. "Our government is taking a wiser and more humane course towards those of the slaves who succeed in getting within the lines of our army," cheered *Douglass' Monthly*.

August 6, 1861: Lincoln signed the First Confiscation Act. It made Butler's decree the law of the land.

April 16, 1862: Lincoln signed a bill that abolished slavery in the District of Columbia. "I trust I am not dreaming," wrote Frederick to Senator Charles Sumner. Frederick wasn't pleased with the law's provision for D.C. slaveholders to be compensated for their human property (up to $300 per person) but he could hardly repudiate this act, which could put close to $1 million into slaveholders' hands, because it liberated about 3,100 children and adults.

July 17, 1862: Lincoln signed two bills that fortified Frederick's faith in the federal government. One (the Militia Act) gave Lincoln the power to let black men serve in the Union Army as laborers and in any other capacity that made sense to Lincoln. It also said that if any of these men were enslaved, they would be declared free. The other law (the Second Confiscation Act) said all black "contraband" would be freed. "At last there is some ground of hope for the slave, and for the country," remarked Frederick to his readers.

Six months later—a thunderbolt. On January 1, 1863, Lincoln issued the Emancipation Proclamation. Blacks enslaved in rebel-held territory were declared free. What's more, black men could now serve as soldiers in the Union Army. The confiscation acts had inspired thousands of blacks, especially in the Upper South, to bolt to Union lines. The Emancipation Proclamation encouraged thousands more to do the same.

"We are all liberated by this proclamation," said Frederick in early February 1863 in the jam-packed great hall of New York

City's Cooper Institute (now Cooper Union). "Everybody is liberated. The white man is liberated, the black man is liberated." This was one of many speeches he delivered that month at Emancipation Proclamation celebrations.

Now that black men could officially serve in the Union Army, Frederick leaped at the chance to be a recruiting agent. In upstate New York, in downstate New York, and elsewhere in the Northeast—"Men of color, to arms!" was his battle cry. In speech after speech, Frederick called on black men to enlist—to prove themselves brave and to liberate their now 4 million brethren in chains. When in New York City, he sometimes worked with Henry Highland Garnet.

> A very large audience assembled last evening [February 6, 1863], in the great hall of the Cooper Institute to listen to perhaps the most eloquent black man in America, on the great questions of the day and of his race, the President's Proclamation of Emancipation and the arming of the black man.
>
> —NEW-YORK DAILY TRIBUNE

From *Harper's Weekly*, February 21, 1863: *The Effects of the Proclamation—Freed Negroes Coming into Our Lines at Newbern, North Carolina*. Depicted here is the day when more than a hundred blacks attached themselves to a Union regiment

in New Bern, North Carolina. "They said that it was known far and wide that the President has declared the slaves free," wrote the soldier who made the drawing on which this engraving is based.

MEN OF COLOR!

TO ARMS! TO ARMS!

NOW OR NEVER

This is our Golden Moment. The Government of the United States calls for every Able-Bodied Colored Man to enter the Army

For Three Years' Service

And join in Fighting the Battles of Liberty and Union.

A MASS MEETING

Of Colored Men, will be held

ON MONDAY, JULY 13,

AT 8 O'CLOCK, AT

CHESTER, DELAWARE CO., PA.

To promote Recruiting Colored Troops for Three Years or the War.

FREDERICK DOUGLASS

And other Distinguished Speakers, will Address the Meeting.

U. S. Steam-power Job Printing Establishment, S. W. Corner of Third and Chestnut Streets, Philada.

WE ARE ALL LIBERATED

Frederick didn't always have the golden touch. Sometimes his soaring oratory prompted only a few black men (or none) to enlist. Still, Frederick was proud of his work. Proud, too, to see his middle son, Frederick Jr., now nineteen, join him as a recruiter. Proud to see Lewis and Charley, twenty-one and seventeen, enlist in the 54th Massachusetts Volunteer Infantry Regiment. They were his first recruits for this regiment, which made a daring but doomed assault on Fort Wagner, on South Carolina's Morris Island, in mid-July 1863. Roughly half the men were wounded, captured, or killed. Lewis, a sergeant major, was among the wounded.

"The grape and canister, shell and minnies swept us down like chaff," Lewis wrote his parents two days after the battle, "still our men went on and on, and if we had been properly supported we would have held the Fort, but the white troops could not be made to come up." (A gravely ill Charley had stayed behind when the 54th marched off to war. He later

The March 1863 issue of *Douglass' Monthly* carried Frederick's editorial, "Men of Color, to Arms!" a passionate plea for black men to join the Union Army—"The day dawns—the morning star is bright upon the horizon! The iron gate of our prison stands half open. One gallant rush from the North will fling it wide open, while four millions of our brothers and sisters shall march out into Liberty!" The title of the editorial was the basis for recruiting posters like this one.

became a first sergeant in the 5th Massachusetts Cavalry.)

The 54th's assault on Fort Wagner wasn't the only instance of black valor, making the Union Army's racist pay policy all the more infuriating. And Frederick had egg on his face.

When recruiting, he had told black men what he had been told: black soldiers would receive the same pay as white soldiers. The War Department, however, had reneged on the deal. Whereas a white private was paid thirteen dollars a month and given free clothing, his black counterpart got *ten* dollars a month and was docked *three* dollars for his pants, sack coat, forage cap, and socks. Also galling: blacks weren't allowed to rise in the ranks into the officer corps.

On August 10, 1863, Frederick went to Washington, D.C., to speak with Lincoln about all this. By his account (Lincoln left no record of the meeting), Frederick was warmly received in the White House and the president listened in earnest to his grievances.

When Frederick left the White House, he did so believing that Lincoln would do something about the grievances of black soldiers. Frederick also believed that he would be the Union Army's first black officer. That's because while there he had also talked with Secretary of War Edwin Stanton. Stanton approached Frederick about serving as assistant adjutant general under General Lorenzo Thomas, who was recruiting blacks in Union-held territory in Mississippi.

What a moment, what a thrill, what a day like no other! The man who as a boy once had a closet floor for a bed had had an audience with—had been listened to by—the president of the United States—and in the White House! And he was poised to become the first black officer in the United States Army! The prospect of a commission, in part, prompted Frederick to close

Storming Fort Wagner (lithograph, 1890). This print applauds the valor of Frederick's son Lewis and other members of the 54th Massachusetts Volunteer Infantry Regiment on July 18, 1863.

shop after sixteen years in the newspaper business. He bade his readers adieu in the August 1863 *Douglass' Monthly*. But never fear, he told them, he would not be tossing his pen or holding his tongue.

Then Frederick waited.

N ot until almost a year later, in June 1864, did the War Department do right by black soldiers on the issue of pay. As for Frederick's commission, it never came. He could still serve under General Thomas, but not as an officer. Insulted, Frederick said no.

The Union wouldn't have its first black officer until February 1865: Frederick's old friend and foe, Martin Delany, was made a major. By then the Union had racked up victory after victory in battles on land and sea. By then General William Tecumseh Sherman had burned Atlanta nearly to the ground, made good on his promise to make Georgia "howl" with his March to the Sea, then had his 60,000-man army wreak havoc in the Carolinas. By the time Delany became a major, the Confederacy was on its last legs, in wreck and ruin. A few months later it waved the white flag. Between battle deaths, disease, and other causes, the war had claimed the lives of more than 600,000 souls, military and civilian. Hundreds of thousands sustained serious wounds.

On Sunday, April 9, 1865, in Appomattox Court House, Virginia, the Confederacy's number one general, Robert E. Lee, surrendered to Ulysses S. Grant, the Union Army's commander in chief. Fighting continued here and there awhile longer, but the Civil War was over.

On April 15 so was Lincoln's life. The president died of a bullet to the brain, put there by Confederate sympathizer John Wilkes Booth the evening before. "The calamity was so sudden," said Frederick in a speech months later, "so out of joint with the prevailing sense of security, involved such a transition from one extreme of feeling to another, from the wildest joy and exultation of victory to the very

Detail from *Abraham Lincoln* (albumen print, 1863). At Lincoln's behest, Frederick returned to the White House in the summer of 1864 to discuss an idea John Brown had called the Subterranean Pass Way. This Underground Railroad on steroids, which wasn't implemented, would have sent squads of black men South to liberate as many of their people as possible. The third and last time Frederick talked with President Lincoln was on March 4, 1865, at a White House reception celebrating Lincoln's second inauguration.

dust and ashes of sorrow and mourning, that few could at first believe it."

When Frederick uttered these words in late December 1865, he and other friends of freedom had celebrated the

The Fall of Richmond, Va. on the Night of April 2d. 1865 (lithograph, 1865). With the imminent arrival of Union troops in defenseless Richmond, the Confederate capital, officials decided to evacuate the city, and some soldiers torched warehouses and other buildings.

abolition of slavery in the United States through the Thirteenth Amendment, officially added to the Constitution on December 18: "Neither slavery nor involuntary servitude, except as a punishment for crime whereof the party shall have been duly convicted, shall exist within the United States, or any place subject to their jurisdiction."

After a quarter century of service to the sacred cause, what would Frederick, nearing fifty, do now?

CHAPTER 7

A New World

"**SLAVERY IS NOT ABOLISHED UNTIL** the black man has the ballot."

That's what Frederick had declared four weeks after Appomattox, on May 10, 1865, in New York City's Church of the Puritans. The occasion was the thirty-second annual meeting of the American Anti-Slavery Society, where William Lloyd Garrison called for the Society's dissolution. With the abolition of slavery a foregone conclusion, the Society's work was done, he contended.

A c. 1865 carte de visite. In early 1864 Frederick switched from beard to walrus mustache.

Frederick had no illusions that in peacetime blacks would suddenly cease to be a despised people. Unless the black man had the vote, Southern states could enact laws to essentially usher in slavery by another name, make freedom "a delusion, a mockery."

Frederick wasn't just worried about the fate of blacks in the South. The North was still steeped in racism, he reminded folks. A case in point: in Illinois, Indiana, and Ohio, blacks still couldn't testify in a court of law against whites. "Where shall the black man look for . . . support, my friends, if the American Anti-Slavery Society fails him?" With Wendell Phillips as president, the Society fought on for black political and civil rights.

W hen speaking out for black suffrage, Frederick had a crisp, biting response to the charge that blacks were not ready for the vote: If the black man "knows enough to pay taxes to support the government, he knows enough to vote; taxation and representation should go together. If he knows enough to shoulder a musket and fight for the flag, fight for the government, he knows enough to vote." Most definitely, Frederick's postwar battle cry was *The vote! The national vote!* at a time when there was so much stacked against his people.

Such as Lincoln's successor, former vice president Andrew Johnson, a Democrat. Once a slaveholder in his native Tennessee, Johnson was an unabashed white supremacist. Shortly after he took the oath of office, he had told a colleague, "This is a country for white men, and by God, as long as I am President, it shall be a government for white men."

To that end, in May 1865 and with Congress not in session, Johnson issued a proclamation of amnesty. To be cleared of the charge of treason, the majority of rebels merely had to pledge allegiance to the United States. Some, including those who owned more than $20,000 in real estate (more than $300,000 today), had to make a personal appeal to the president for a pardon. (Before long, legions of "$20,000 men" were pardoned.)

In a second proclamation Johnson revealed to Frederick and the world how lenient he would be when it came to Reconstruction, the process by which ex-Confederate states were readmitted to the Union. He started with North Carolina. After appointing Democrat William Holden its provisional governor, Johnson had him hold a state convention to create a new state constitution that repealed the ordinance of secession and ratified the Thirteenth Amendment. Only white men could vote for convention delegates.

By fall 1865, with the exception of Texas (which wouldn't ratify the Thirteenth Amendment until 1870), every former rebel state was back in the Union. Worse, former Confederate states had instituted—or were poised to institute—"Black Codes": laws to subjugate blacks just as before. There were pass systems and curfews. There were bans against blacks earning livelihoods as blacksmiths and other artisans. If authorities deemed black parents too poor to raise their kids, they could force the children into apprenticeships (up to the age of twenty-one for boys and eighteen for girls). Vicious, too, was the convict lease system, through which blacks jailed, often on trumped-up charges, could be rented out to work on plantations and other white enterprises.

Just as Frederick feared.

Slavery by another name.

The vote! The national vote!

For most black Southerners the only help close at hand was the Bureau of Refugees, Freedmen, and Abandoned Lands. This social service agency, headed by Union General Oliver O. Howard, was known as the Freedmen's Bureau because most of its clients had been enslaved. These people looked to the bureau for shelter, food, clothing, medical care, jobs—protection.

The vote! The national vote!

A c. 1863 ambrotype. Frederick especially had in mind men like the one seen here when he agitated for black male suffrage. This unidentified Union soldier poses with his wife and daughters (in matching hats and coats).

Even when a speech wasn't explicitly about suffrage, Frederick often brought up the issue. He did this in Baltimore in the fall of 1865, at the dedication of an institution devoted to black educational, social, and cultural uplift and named in his honor: the Douglass Institute. It was located in a building on Baltimore's East Lexington Street once occupied by Newton University, a building a group of blacks had purchased for $16,000. As "dismal as is the hour, troubled and convulsed as

the times, we may congratulate ourselves upon the establishment of this institution," said Frederick on dedication day. The
Institute came at the right time, a time when the issue of suffrage was being hotly debated. It was just the thing to counter
allegations of black inferiority and "incapacity." And Frederick was hopeful that the white people of the North would do
the right thing—if not out of sheer decency then out of self-
preservation: to keep the Old South from roaring back. "They
gave us the bullet to save themselves; they will yet give the
ballot to save themselves." This was just a few weeks before
Connecticut voters rejected a proposal to add black suffrage to
their state's constitution. Fortunately for Frederick and like-
minded folk, there were whites in high places champing at the
bit to make serious changes. Enter the Radical Republicans.

Because so many Democrats in Congress had joined the
Confederacy, the Republican party controlled Congress
during and after the war. Within that party there was
a dynamic and resolute group known as the Radicals: abolitionists intent on empowering black people and punishing the
states that had rebelled. Outraged over what Johnson had
done, when Congress came back into session in December

1865, Senator Charles Sumner, Pennsylvania representative Thaddeus Stevens, and other Radicals were determined to wrest Reconstruction out of his hands. For starters, they saw to it that Congress refused to seat senators and representatives from states readmitted under Johnson's plan. These states were basically kicked out of the Union.

While Radicals worked on new, progressive legislation, Frederick kept on with his battle cry. In early February 1866 he headed a delegation of black men who secured a meeting with President Johnson, with everyone's remarks made available to the press.

This delegation included Frederick's son Lewis; John Jones of Chicago; William Whipper, a successful entrepreneur from Pennsylvania; and George T. Downing, proprietor of a hotel and catering business in Newport, Rhode Island, and manager of the House of Representatives dining room. The group's goal was twofold: to protest the virtually nonexistent enforcement of the Thirteenth Amendment, and to urge the president to support black suffrage. "You enfranchise your enemies and disfranchise your friends," said Frederick to Johnson, trying to get him to see that as things stood, most black Southerners lived at the mercy of whites just as in slavery. His lead argument, however, was this: If black men could be taxed and drafted, and have other obligations to the government, how then could they be deprived of the vote? Nothing Frederick or anyone else said moved Johnson, who blathered on about how giving the black man the ballot would lead to a race war. He also suggested that perhaps blacks should just leave the country. After the delegation left, the president railed against and cursed Frederick and the other black men to his private secretary.

The widely publicized meeting between the dignified delegation and the vulgar president generated support for Frederick's new sacred cause in the halls of Congress and on the street. Radical Republicans were ready to take more action.

April 9, 1866: Over Johnson's veto, Congress passed a

> **It would be hard to surpass the brief address of Frederick Douglass for fitness to the occasion and point. It would be hard to find a worse speech than the diffuse, illogical, clumsy, and coarse reply of the president."**
>
> —NATIONAL ANTI-SLAVERY STANDARD

civil rights bill to counter the Black Codes—all people born in the United States, except for Native Americans living on reservations, were now citizens of the United States and entitled to federal protection of their lives and property.

President Johnson's well-known courtesy and self-possession were put to the test today by the visitation of Frederick Douglass at the head of the great colored delegation from the Northern cities. . . . Mr. Douglass spoke as if he was upon equal terms with Mr. Johnson. . . . The President stood his ground manfully, and yet modestly. . . . The President said, in substance, that if the freedmen were allowed suffrage it would be destructive to the interests of the blacks and the whites.

—RICHMOND EXAMINER

June 13, 1866: Congress passed the Fourteenth Amendment to cement black citizenship—"All persons born or naturalized in the United States, and subject to the jurisdiction thereof, are citizens of the United States and of the state wherein they reside." The amendment also disqualified anyone who had resigned their civil or military post to join the Confederacy from holding a federal or state office, with the proviso that Congress could lift the ban (which it did in stages and completely in 1898). As well, the Fourteenth Amendment made a state's representation in Congress contingent on the number of male voters age twenty-one and older. If a state denied black men the vote, it would have fewer representatives (and in several Southern states blacks outnumbered whites). This amendment, like all others, then had to be ratified by three-quarters of the states.

January 8, 1867: Congress granted D.C.'s male residents, twenty-one years or older, the right to vote. (Exceptions included paupers and men with convictions for serious crimes.)

March 2, 1867: Over Johnson's veto Congress passed the First Reconstruction Act. The ex-rebel states were reduced to conquered territory and put under military rule. Ratification of the Fourteenth Amendment was now a condition of readmission into the Union. (The exception was Tennessee. Back in July 1866 it had ratified this amendment and so was back in the Union.)

During these days of sweeping changes, *The vote! The national vote!* remained Frederick's battle cry.

When in July 1868 the Fourteenth Amendment became a part of the Constitution—

The vote! The national vote!

As some Northern states granted black men the vote without property qualifications and others denied it—

The vote! The national vote!

Finally on February 26, 1869, Congress passed the Fifteenth Amendment: U.S. citizens could not be denied the state or federal vote "on account of race, color, or previous condition of servitude" (but not gender).

Yes! Yes!

For his support of the Fifteenth Amendment Frederick faced the fury of some feminists, more than a few of them friends. When urged to stand instead for universal suffrage—the national vote for men *and* women—

I can't! I can't!

Frederick still supported women's suffrage. But he was a realist. Universal suffrage didn't have a chance at the time. He also maintained that it was more imperative for black men to have the vote—that racism was a worse scourge and more deadly than sexism.

Frederick explained himself most passionately in May 1869 in New York City, at the first annual meeting of the American

Equal Rights Association (AERA): "With us, the [suffrage] matter is a question of life and death, at least in fifteen States of the Union. When women, because they are women, are hunted down through the cities of New York and New Orleans; when they are dragged from their houses and hung upon lamp-posts; when their children are torn from their arms, and their brains dashed upon the pavement; when they are objects of insult and outrage at every turn; when they are in danger of having their homes burnt down over their heads; when their children are not allowed to enter schools; then they will have an urgency to obtain the ballot equal to our own."

When an audience member asked didn't these horrible things happen to black women, too—

"Yes, yes, yes; it is true of

> **Think of Patrick and Sambo and Hans and Yung Tung who do not know the difference between a Monarchy and a Republic, who never read the Declaration of Independence or Webster's spelling book, making laws for Lydia Maria Child, Lucretia Mott, or Fanny Kemble.**
>
> **—ELIZABETH CADY STANTON**, disgusted over the possibility of immigrant and black men getting the national vote before educated, accomplished white women

Representative Women (lithograph c. 1870). These seven white reformers are (*clockwise from top*): Lucretia Mott, AERA's first president; Elizabeth Cady Stanton; Mary Ashton Rice Livermore, who helped form the Civil War–era equivalent of the Red Cross; Lydia Maria Child, writer and editor; Susan B. Anthony; and Sara Jane Clarke Lippincott, better known by her pen name, Grace Greenwood, the *New York Times*' first woman journalist. *Center*: famed orator Anna Elizabeth Dickinson.

the black woman, but not because she is a woman, but because she is black."

In his AERA address Frederick wasn't being overdramatic. Violence against blacks and their white allies was epidemic, especially in the former Confederate states—even with federal troops stationed down there. White supremacist outfits such as the Ku Klux Klan killed and maimed, burned down homes and schools. Back in May 1866 it was mostly black blood that flowed in Memphis, Tennessee, during a three-day white riot against blacks in and out of uniform. Over 40 dead. Two months after the Memphis Riot about the same number of blacks died in the New Orleans Riot. And that was not the end of the troubles in Louisiana. Eight months before Frederick spoke at the AERA convention, in September 1868, there was the Opelousas Massacre, which some sources say ended the lives of about 150 blacks while others put the death toll at about 300.

After the war, the Freedmen's Bureau's files bulged with reports of white-on-black indiscriminate savagery: People were beaten, bludgeoned, beheaded. In one case a black man was attacked because he was too ill to work. Another was shot dead because he failed to tip his hat when passing by a white man.

The North was no stranger to such barbarism. One of the nation's worst riots ever had occurred during the summer of 1863 in New York City, when a white protest against the draft turned violent. After four days of madness and mayhem in the New York City Draft Riots, with blacks the number one targets, more than 100 people were dead and some 2,000 injured.

When Frederick, by now fifty-one, spoke at the AERA convention in May 1869, thirteen states had ratified the Fifteenth Amendment. Another fifteen were needed to meet the three-fourths requirement for an amendment to be added to the Constitution.

The wait lasted through the summer and fall and into the winter of 1870. It ended on March 30, 1870, the day the Fifteenth Amendment was adopted into the Constitution! "Henceforth we live in a new world," declared Frederick a month later at a celebration of the amendment in Albany's Tweddle Hall, filled to capacity. "At last, at last, the black man has a future."

By then ten of the eleven former Confederate states were back in the Union. Georgia, the exception, would be, too, that summer.

And in this new world, Frederick had a new newspaper.

CHAPTER 8

Promises in Your Constitution

N LATE SUMMER 1870 FREDERICK took over an eight-month-old struggling black-owned D.C. weekly, the *New Era*. Renaming it the *New National Era*, he geared up to spend a lot of time in the capital, about three hundred miles away from Rochester. And wife Anna.

The *New National Era*, at 418 11th Street NW, reported on the ongoing Franco-Prussian war, the national debt, and a debate over polygamy in Utah, among other things in its first issue, September 8, 1870. It also carried updates on public figures. Richard

Carte de visite, c. 1871: Frederick was especially fond of the profile pose.

T. Greener, the first black Harvard graduate (1870) and in his twenties, was still on his sickbed in Boston. Gerrit Smith, in his seventies and long since out of that insane asylum, was using his "well preserved mental and moral faculties" in the temperance movement. The paper invited Martin Delany to drop a line.

In the *New National Era*, as in his speeches, Frederick urged hard work and thrift, rallying blacks to amass money, to spend

Smithsonian Institution Building from Pennsylvania Ave, 1874 (photographic print, 1874). The view is toward the south from the corner of Pennsylvania and 11th Street. Among the businesses seen here on the right are Latimer & Cleary auction house and the Star Buildings, home to a paper Frederick took: the *Evening Star*.

not on excessive finery and frivolity but on homes, businesses, and income-producing investments. He called on his people to do as he had done. And most definitely he had come a very long way.

In slavery, Frederick's captors made money off him and during those early days of freedom his wages were meager—that is, until he embarked on a career as a lecturer, earning on average $450 a year for about a hundred engagements in the 1840s.

The tall building on the left is Harvey's, one of the city's most famous restaurants. Frederick's *New National Era*, at 418 11th Street, NW, is behind Harvey's. In the distance looms the Smithsonian "castle."

By the late 1850s he typically charged $25 per speech. In the 1870s that fee generally ranged from $75 to $125, and Frederick earned thousands of dollars a year—sometimes one thousand in less than a month, as happened in early December 1872. For ten talks in upstate New York, western Pennsylvania, Ohio, Wisconsin, and Illinois, before the ten percent commission to his agent and longtime friend James Redpath, Frederick earned $1,000 (nearly $20,000 today). Over the years Frederick had also invested in real estate as well as in stocks and bonds.

Given how well Frederick did for himself, it's no wonder that one of his favorite and most popular speeches was "Self-Made Men," a salute to people who began life with nothing and made something of themselves through—not connections, not luck—but hard work when given half a chance. Self-improvement and amassing wealth were not an end but a means. Self-made men (and women) were duty bound, he believed, to use their abilities and resources to improve their worlds.

It must have saddened Frederick that his own children, none of whom went to college, weren't more successful. After the war Lewis and Frederick Jr. had pursued various endeavors in Denver, Colorado, then in the nation's capital, but were stymied. One way Frederick came to their aid was

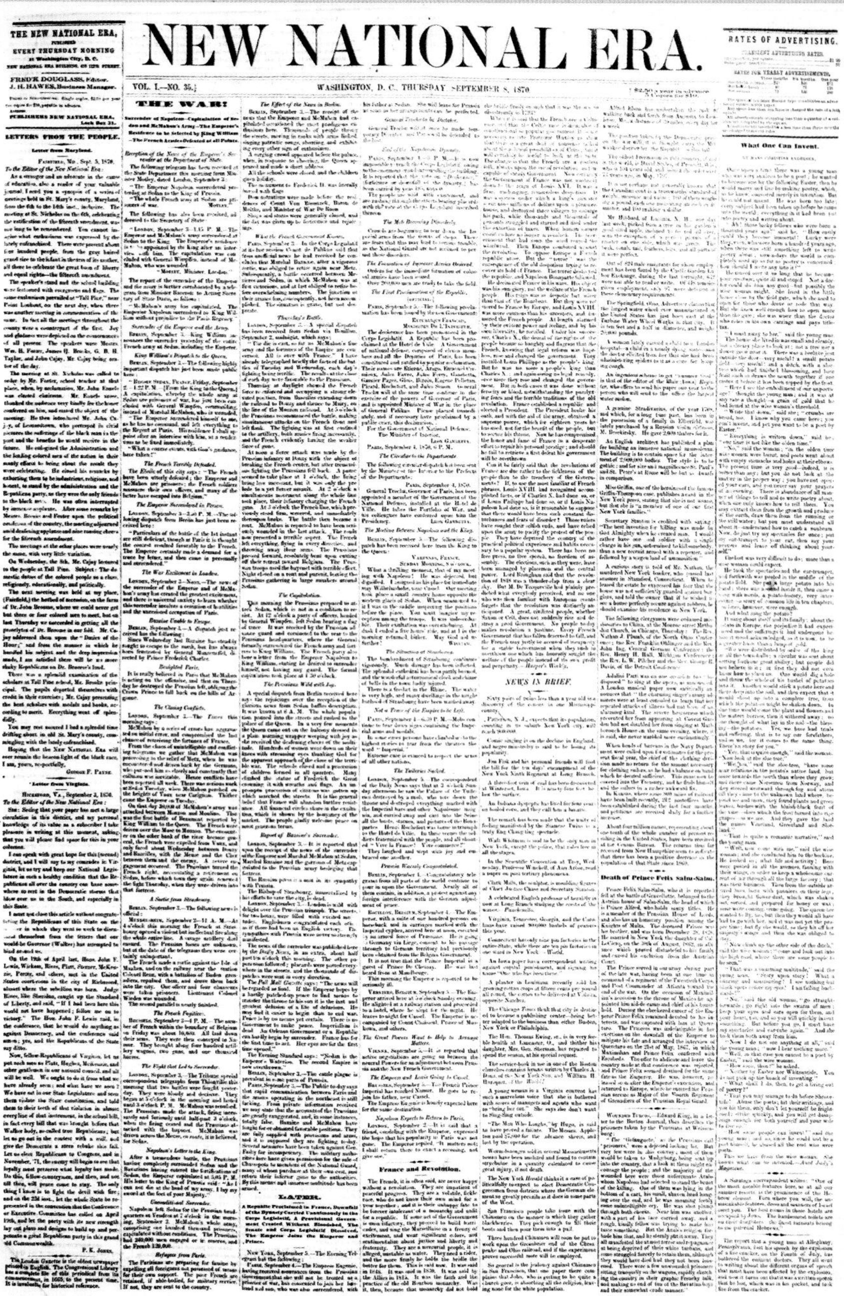

THE NEW NATIONAL ERA,
PUBLISHED
EVERY THURSDAY MORNING
at Washington City, D. C.

FRED'K DOUGLASS, Editor.
J. H. HAWES, Business Manager.

PUBLISHED NEW NATIONAL ERA.

NEW NATIONAL ERA.

RATES OF ADVERTISING.

VOL. I.—NO. 35.]   WASHINGTON, D. C., THURSDAY SEPTEMBER 8, 1870.

THE WAR!

by turning the *New National Era* over to them in 1873. By then both were married. While Lewis was not to have any children, Frederick Jr. would have seven and often ask his father for financial help.

Charley, also a husband and father, had several government jobs, including as a clerk for the Freedmen's Bureau and for the Treasury Department. But he, who like his mother was rather sickly, often turned to his father when in debt.

As for "the pulse" of Frederick's heart, during the war Rosetta had married Nathan Sprague, a member of the 54th Massachusetts, who had been born into slavery. After the war Rosetta's husband tried his hand at farming, at hack driving, at this, at that. Nothing worked out for him. Frederick came to their rescue, too. Sometimes with money. Sometimes by letting them and their children live in his home.

1. Frederick and Anna's youngest son, Charles Remond (carte de visite, date unknown). Like his father, Charley had a passion for the violin, a passion his son Joseph would also develop.

2. Frederick and Anna's second son, Frederick Jr., (carte de visite, date unknown).

3. Frederick and Anna's oldest son, Lewis Henry (carte de visite, date unknown). Beside him is his wife, Helen, daughter of Frederick's friend the Reverend Jermain Wesley Loguen.

4. Frederick and Anna's oldest child, Rosetta Sprague, (carte de visite, date unknown).

Rosetta, her husband, and their three children were living in her parents' home on the night of Sunday, June 2, 1872, when a fire broke out. After everyone was safely out of the house, they tried, with the help of neighbors, to get as many of their belongings as they could out onto the lawn.

When Frederick arrived from Washington the next day, he faced utter devastation. The house, the barn and other outbuildings, coaches, buggies, everything but the horses Rosetta's husband managed to save—destroyed. "Scarcely a trace of the building, except brick walls and stone foundations, is left," Frederick informed *New National Era* readers of his home. In a piece for a Rochester paper, he mourned the trees he had planted some twenty years earlier, "scorched and charred beyond recovery."

A piano worth $500 was among the items saved but "much damaged." Frederick calculated that even after insurance he lost $4,000 to $5,000 (about $100,000 today). Complete sets of his first three newspapers were among the priceless losses. When Frederick learned that firefighters suspected arson, he was livid, even more wounded—and soon done with Rochester, his home for twenty-five years.

Frederick moved his family to Washington, D.C. Home was now a town house on Capitol Hill, at 316 A Street NE, a home he expanded in the fall of 1873 by buying the adjoining house and breaking down the wall that divided the properties.

About two years after he settled in the capital, where he bought a gold watch at Mermod and Jacquard Jewelry Company and clothing at Wm. S. Teel's men's shop, had shirts made at Philip T. Hall's, and got gaiters at J. J. Georges' shoe shop, Frederick was tapped to be president of the Freedman's Savings and Trust Company, better known as Freedman's Bank, which

Frederick Douglass in Front of His A Street NE Home (albumen print, 1878). To the right is Frederick in top hat and suit; on the far right is Rosetta and one of her daughters.

Congress had created back in March 1865. Initially intended to help black servicemen rise in life, this bank, run by white men, attracted the pennies, nickels, dimes, and dollars of an array of black people. When Frederick, one of the bank's boosters, became its president in March 1874, the bank had more than thirty branches in about a dozen states and the District of Columbia. Frederick's job came with a fancy office in a new four-story stone building on Pennsylvania Avenue, across the street from the White House. But all that glitters . . .

At the start, the Freedman's Bank was limited to making safe and secure investments with depositors' money. But in time the men who oversaw it began making riskier investments to earn a higher rate of interest. Those investments included stock in railroad companies, many of which went belly up, triggering an economic downturn that started in September 1873. In the Panic of 1873, the first worldwide economic depression, thousands of businesses failed—including scores of banks, because of investment losses and because of people rushing to withdraw their money.

Why did Frederick, who knew nothing about banking, take the job—six months after the depression began? Did he believe his prestige would inspire great confidence in the bank? How

The Department of Justice (Freedman's Bank Building) by unidentified photographer, a photographic copy of a c. 1880 wood engraving.

much did he know about the bank's state of affairs before he said yes?

In late June 1874, the *New National Era* carried his letter to the bank's customers (of which he was one). The bad news: at the start of the year, the bank's debts exceeded its assets by more than $200,000 (over $4 million today). The good news: the bank had sworn off risky investments and put a freeze on opening new branches. Cost-cutting measures included reducing some salaries. The bank would not only survive, it would "flourish." Frederick either was delusional or had been duped. On July 2 the bank shut its doors. Some 61,000 people, with deposits ranging on average from five dollars to fifty, lost a total of nearly $3.3 million. In years to come about half of those people would recoup some money but not the full amount: about $540,000 as a group. Because of what happened to the Freedman's Bank, for years many blacks lived with a deep distrust of banks, preferring to keep their money tucked under a mattress or inside a tin can or cigar box stashed in a hideaway.

Three months after the Freedman's Bank closed, the *New National Era* was shuttered. Despite Frederick's periodic cash infusions, his sons hadn't been able to make the paper profitable.

After the Freedman's Bank and the *New National Era*

failed, Frederick didn't retreat from public life. On he surged, still a much sought-after speaker. And there was plenty to rail against.

Southern barbarism was still rampant despite enforcement acts President Ulysses S. Grant, a Republican, signed into law in the early 1870s. Known as the Ku Klux Klan Acts, they made it a federal crime to interfere with a person's rights, especially the right to vote. Still, white violence against blacks—to keep them from exercising their rights, to keep them from pursuing dreams and aspirations, to keep them from living normal lives—continued with a vengeance. In Louisiana there was the Colfax Massacre on Easter Sunday, April 13, 1873, and the Coushatta Massacre on August 25, 1874. Months later, on December 7, in Mississippi there was the Vicksburg Massacre.

One ray of light came on March 1, 1875. President Grant signed off on a civil rights bill Senator Charles Sumner had introduced years earlier. This law made it a crime for hotels, theaters, and other places of public accommodations to discriminate against people because of their race, color, or previous condition of servitude. Those who violated the Civil Rights Act of 1875 could be fined between $500 and $1,000 or jailed for thirty days.

J ust as Frederick had stumped for Lincoln in 1860 and 1864, and for Grant in 1868 and 1872, so, too, did he stump for the Republican Party's presidential candidate, Ohio Governor Rutherford B. Hayes, in the year of the nation's centennial. Hayes' opponent was the Democrat Samuel Tilden, governor of New York.

At the Republican National Convention in Cincinnati, Ohio, in June 1876, Frederick held the party's feet to the fire in his address in Exposition Hall. "You say you have emancipated us. You have; and I thank you for it. You say you have enfranchised us. You have; and I thank you for it. But what is your emancipation?—what is your enfranchisement? What does it all amount to, if the black man, after having been made free by the letter of your law, is unable to exercise that freedom, and, after having been freed from the slaveholder's lash, he is to be subject to the slaveholder's shot-gun?" Despite the laws enacted during Reconstruction, blacks were still orphans of the storm. "Do you mean to make good to us the promises in your constitution?" Frederick thundered.

From *Frank Leslie's Illustrated News*, July 1, 1876: *Ohio—The Republican National Convention at Cincinnati, June 14th, 15th and 16th* (engraving). The convention was held in Exposition Hall.

While millions of blacks saw no change for the better in their lives, Frederick received a prestigious post. About two weeks after Rutherford B. Hayes' inauguration in March 1877, the president appointed Frederick U.S. Marshal of the District of Columbia with oversight of the arrest of thieves and other lawbreakers. A first for a black person.

There is no man living that I should so rejoice to see hold this position at the Capital of the Nation as yourself.

—**HARRIET JACOBS**, writer, activist, and former resident of Rochester, at that time residing in Cambridge, Massachusetts. Born in slavery in North Carolina, she had made it to free soil in 1842.

About a month after Hayes made Frederick a marshal, he pulled the remaining troops out of the South (in South Carolina and Louisiana). He was keeping his part of the bargain made in the contested election of 1876 that included charges of ballot box stuffing in parts of the South. Hayes became the president after political operatives made a backroom deal: in exchange for the presidency he'd remove troops from the South and end federal intervention there. He'd end Reconstruction.

The First Colored Senator and Representatives—in the 41st and 42nd Congress of the United States (lithograph, 1872). Standing (*left to right*): Representatives Robert Carlos DeLarge of South Carolina and Jefferson Franklin Long of Georgia. Seated, (*left to right*): Senator Hiram Revels of Mississippi and Representatives Benjamin Sterling Turner of Alabama, Josiah Walls of Florida, Joseph Hayne Rainey of South Carolina, and Robert Brown Elliott, also of South Carolina.

The Republican Party was not making good on the Constitution's promises. How could blacks hold on to their rights now? During Reconstruction some six hundred black men had served in state legislatures. Fifteen had served in Congress. After the Compromise of 1877 the nation would not see numbers like that again for decades.

Some people thought Frederick should resign as marshal given what Hayes did and also because he was stripped of a traditional duty of a D.C. marshal: introducing dignitaries to the president in the White House. Despite the betrayal (and the snub), Frederick remained loyal to the Republican Party and campaigned for its next presidential candidate, James Garfield, another Ohioan who defeated Democrat Winfield Scott Hancock, a Pennsylvanian, in the 1880 election.

President Garfield didn't reappoint Frederick as D.C. marshal but gave him the less prestigious post of recorder of deeds: keeper of the district's real estate–related records and documents. Like other officeholders, Frederick wasn't above nepotism, handing out jobs to relatives and friends. Daughter Rosetta and sons Lewis and Frederick Jr. were among his clerks at one point. So was Rosetta's husband, after serving a year

> We believe that the craze for [holding] office is our bane. It has turned the heads of Frederick Douglass and John M. Langston [U.S. minister to Haiti]. Let us hope that Richard T. Greener will keep his head level and himself free from entanglements.

—D.C.'s black-owned weekly *PEOPLE'S ADVOCATE* on rumors that Richard T. Greener, dean of Howard University's law school, was to be a member of President Garfield's cabinet in prison for mail tampering while he was a postal worker in Rochester. Another hire was Helen Pitts, daughter of the white couple Gideon and Jane Pitts of Honeoye, New York, Frederick's former fellow conductors on the Underground Railroad. Helen, a graduate of today's Mount Holyoke College, had moved to D.C. in 1880. Early on she stayed with an uncle, one of Frederick's neighbors.

By then Frederick no longer lived on Capitol Hill but across the Anacostia River in the suburb of Uniontown (renamed Anacostia in 1886). Frederick's new home, high up on a hill, was a fifteen-acre estate with gardens and a croquet court among other splendors. Its white-frame Southern Gothic mansion would eventually have twenty-one rooms. The view of the capital from Frederick's place, which he named Cedar Hill, was magnificent.

It was almost always open house at Cedar Hill. A lot of people lived there, too, in the late 1870s: Rosetta and her five girls and one son (with her husband off in Omaha trying to make a go of another business, a bakery); Charley, now a widower, and his several children; and someone with whom Frederick had reunited after the war, his brother, Perry, who had taken the last name Downs.

Snow at Cedar Hill in 1887 (unknown type of photograph). The young man (*far right*) might be one of Frederick's grandchildren. This photograph was taken by his son Charley on February 27, 1887.

When Frederick lived in Rochester, he had built a small cottage on his land where Perry and his family lived for two years before moving back to Maryland. Years later, when Perry, five years older than Frederick, came to Cedar Hill with a daughter, he was dying. "I am glad to have a shelter for him,"

Frederick wrote a friend in April 1879. Perry died in 1880, sometime after June when the census showed him living with Frederick, as were several granddaughters, a nephew, Nathan Sprague's sister, Louisa, Frederick's sister Kitty, and a servant.

Perhaps the most frequent visitor to Cedar Hill was Ottilie Assing, a journalist for a German newspaper who had translated *My Bondage and My Freedom* into German. Some historians maintain that this woman, who stayed at Cedar Hill for weeks at a time, was Frederick's mistress for more than twenty years. Others contend that the affair was a figment of this mentally unstable woman's imagination.

O f all the rooms in Cedar Hill, undoubtedly Frederick's favorite was his study/library adorned with images of luminaries and other accoutrements of Victorian bourgeois culture and, of course, with books, books, books!—from travel books and histories to grammar books and collections of sermons and speeches.

When it came to current events, Frederick had subscriptions to a mix of black- and white-owned periodicals, from D.C.'s *Evening Star*, the *Washington Post*, and the *Christian Recorder* to New York City's *Freeman*, the *Woman's Journal* out of Boston, and *Anti-Caste*, a journal promoting brother-hood published in Somerset, England. Not surprisingly, Frederick was quite the joiner, with memberships in organizations as different as the Republican National League, the National Woman Suffrage Association, and the American Peace Society. He was a giver, too. Virginia's Manassas Industrial School for Colored Youth and the Washington Free Kindergarten were among the charities he supported over the years while living at Cedar Hill.

Detail from *Anna M. Douglass* (painting, 1922, based on a photograph). Born about 1813, Anna was the daughter of Mary and Bambarra Murray, who were freed from slavery shortly before she was born on Maryland's Eastern Shore, in Denton. Anna moved seventy miles to Baltimore as a young woman and supported herself as a housekeeper and laundress.

During his days at Cedar Hill, Frederick worked on his third autobiography, bringing his life up-to-date with the nearly six-hundred-page *Life and Times of Frederick Douglass*, published in the fall of 1881, when he was sixty-three.

Less than a year later tragedy struck at Cedar Hill. Anna suffered a severe stroke that paralyzed her left side. A few weeks later, on Wednesday, August 4, 1882, Frederick's wife of forty-four years died. According to her death certificate she was sixty-nine years old.

After the death of his demure, dutiful, apparently never demanding wife, Frederick was adrift. Maybe move to Europe? Maybe . . . He faced hard days ahead. Hard physically, emotionally, mentally. Shortly before the one-year anniversary of Anna's death, he was in such a bad way that friends hustled him off for a rest in Poland Springs, a resort town in Maine. When Frederick returned, he was rejuvenated. And he wasn't a widower for much longer.

She was his employee. She was twenty years younger. And she was white. Jaws dropped when word spread that on the evening of Thursday, January 24, 1884, Frederick married one of his clerks, Helen Pitts. They were married in a private ceremony in the home of the Reverend Francis J. Grimké, pastor of one of the city's most prominent black churches, Fifteenth Street Presbyterian Church. The minister's wife, Charlotte Forten Grimké, and two people in their home were the only witnesses. Frederick's children learned of the impending marriage only hours before.

For remarrying—and to a white woman—Frederick faced their rage. And that of other blacks, too.

Fred Douglass . . . has made the fatal error of his life. He has forfeited his claim to the leadership of his race by a foolish and unwise step.

—the black-owned *PILOT* of Birmingham, Alabama

We have no further use for him as a leader. His picture hangs in our parlor; we will hang it in the stable.

—the black-owned *PITTSBURGH WEEKLY NEWS*

The friends of our genial, great-hearted sage will unite in wishing him many years of married felicity.

—the black-owned *CONSERVATOR* of Chicago, Illinois

His marriage will not impair his grand eloquence and preeminent qualities of mind and character, and his influence and usefulness in behalf of humanity will continue in full force.

—the *AFRO-AMERICAN* of Cincinnati, Ohio

Helen Pitts Douglass (unknown type of photograph, c. 1880). While in Washington, D.C., Helen coedited with another white woman, Dr. Caroline B. Winslow, the *Alpha*, a monthly magazine published by the city's Moral Education Society. This photograph was taken about four years before Helen Pitts became Helen Pitts Douglass.

CHAPTER 9

Leaf from a Living Tree

IAM WRITING YOU ON THE [EVE OF THE] seventh anniversary of my last marriage," Frederick remarked in a letter to Rosetta from Port-au-Prince, Haiti, on January 23, 1891. He recalled the attacks heaped upon him for marrying Helen, especially from blacks who made him out to be "a traitor to my race, as if I belonged to one race more than to another. . . . Happily their hard words did not kill me."

Frederick Douglass at His Desk in Haiti (albumen print, c. 1890). Frederick is not asleep but engrossed in a book in the room that served as his office while he lived in Villa Tivoli in Port-au-Prince, Haiti. Helen recalled that during their time in Haiti, many nights Frederick got out of bed to "stand beneath the open sky & commune with the stars."

During those seven years Frederick's children never warmed to Helen—they called her "Mrs. Douglass"—but they, especially Rosetta, couldn't stop loving their father.

As for the controversial couple, several months after they married, they went on a honeymoon, visiting more than a dozen cities in the Midwest, upstate New York, and New England. They went to the Thousand Islands of the St. Lawrence River and Montreal, too. Less than two years later, in 1886, and with Frederick no longer D.C.'s recorder of deeds, the couple took an even bigger trip, which Frederick could well afford. Not counting Cedar Hill, his assets were valued at $85,000 (about $2.2 million today).

A t two oclk, or there about, the mountain coasts of dear old Ireland . . . came into view," Frederick scribbled in his diary on Wednesday, September 22, 1886. A few hours later the steamer *City of Rome* docked at Queenstown Harbor, where he and Helen boarded a boat that took them across the Irish Sea to Liverpool. Their grand tour began!

"Oct. 1st: We have now spent a week in Liverpool, have visited the art galleries, the Free Library . . ."

"Arrived in Paris Wednesday 20th October 1886 and rode to the Hotel Britanique . . ."

"Jan 13: Arrived in Marseilles last night too dark to get a view of the blue waters of the Mediteranian [*sic*]."

"Jan 15th: Took train for Nice . . . Spent but one day here and pushed on through Mentone and several other interesting towns to Genova."

"Jan. 18th: Came to the old town of Pisa, saw the Leaning Tower."

January 19, 1887, was one of the grandest days—they arrived in Rome, the Eternal City. Frederick was speechless as he stood beneath the dome of St. Peter's Basilica.

Naples was next. Then nearby Pompeii, buried by nearly ten feet of ash and pumice when Mount Vesuvius erupted in 79 CE.

On Tuesday, February 8, the couple headed to the coastal town of Amalfi. Frederick declared the winding road "an ingeneering triumph." He noted that "little and large vessels dot the whole coast with their white sails." Unlike when he was a boy standing on the banks of Chesapeake Bay, the sight of these sails didn't bring him to tears, but was a "constant delight to the eye."

During their travels, Frederick and Helen stayed in fine hotels and dined in great restaurants. They visited old friends of his, such as Julia Griffiths Crofts, now a widow, when in England. When in Rome Charles Remond's three sisters, one of whom had a medical practice there. Frederick and Helen also visited friends of friends and made new friends. And they stayed on the go. Except on rainy days. Those were prime times for Frederick to write letters to family, who wouldn't see him again for some time.

"We decided to day to extend our visit to Egypt and Greece," Frederick wrote in his diary on February 11, 1887. "It is no small thing to see the land of Joseph and his brethren and from which Moses led the children of Abraham out of the house of Bondage."

Bondage. That was how he began in life. Given that, he mused, what a strange and wonderful thing "that I should be plowing this classic sea and on my way to the land of Moses and the Pharaohs." This was on the night of February 14, his adopted birthday, chosen because his mother had called him her little valentine. "Aside from a cold and a little hint of sea sickness, I am quite well, strong, and cheerful," he wrote.

And plow on he did.

Mr. Frederick Douglass has just returned to London after nine months of travel on the continent and in Egypt. He will probably remain in England several months before returning home. . . . "It was here," said Mr. Douglass, "that forty-one years ago I received the bill of sale of my own body. . . . The money was [raised] by two sisters, Ellen and Anna Richardson, living at Newcastle-on-Tyne. . . . One is 79 and the other over 80 years old." Mr. Douglass intends to visit these ladies in a few days.

—*KANSAS CITY STAR*

In Egypt he visited mosques and tombs. He made the more than four-hundred-foot climb—at age sixty-nine!—up the Great Pyramid of Giza. He and Helen also enjoyed a five-day sail up Africa's legendary Nile River. In Alexandria, Frederick marveled at the site where the world's largest library once stood.

The Acropolis and the Parthenon were among the sights they drank in when the couple reached Athens, Greece. After a few days there, they headed back to Italy, back to France, then on to England, arriving there in late spring 1887.

Helen had to cut her trip short. Her mother was very ill. Frederick was acutely aware that Helen's father wouldn't let him set foot into his house—that's how much this abolitionist loathed the fact that his daughter had married a black man—and so Frederick remained in England giving lectures, visiting friends, and frequenting museums, art galleries, and the like. Before the summer was out, both he and Helen were back at Cedar Hill.

D uring those seven years of his second marriage, Frederick continued to be a force. Continued to lecture. Continued to write. Continued to try to get people to see that humanity is one the world over. Continued to be the de facto president of black America.

Frederick also continued to lament the ground the nation had lost in the aftermath of Reconstruction. In the 1880s that loss included the Civil Rights Act of 1875: In October 1883, the U.S. Supreme Court declared it unconstitutional because only state and local governments—not Congress—could legislate against a park or hotel having discriminatory practices. The high court's decision put the country on a course for entrenched segregation.

"It has swept over the land like a moral cyclone, leaving

moral desolation in its track," said Frederick at a meeting in D.C.'s Lincoln Hall a week after the ruling. "We feel it, as we felt the furious attempt, years ago, to force the accursed system of slavery upon the soil of Kansas, the enactment of the Fugitive Slave Bill, the repeal of the Missouri Compromise, the Dred Scott decision. I look upon it as one more shocking development of that moral weakness in high places which has attended the conflict between the spirit of liberty and the spirit of slavery from the beginning, and I venture to predict that it will be so regarded by after-coming generations."

Six years later seventy-one-year-old Frederick vowed to keep fighting the good fight at his surprise birthday party hosted by Washington's Bethel Literary Society. "With the help of God," he told the crowd, "while life shall endure, you shall find me faithful in the support of every movement and measure looking to the enlightenment and improvement of our yet much oppressed, abused, and slandered people."

A year and a half later the man called the Sage of Anacostia, or the Lion of Anacostia, found himself about to embark on a very different mission. In June 1889 President Benjamin Harrison appointed Frederick minister resident and consul general of Haiti. This time there was no Southern storm to keep him from going to Haiti (though he did have to wait for some civil unrest there to die down before he made the journey). That's why his "Dear Rose," as he called his daughter, received a letter from him on January 23, 1891, from the Haitian capital, Port-au-Prince, where Frederick and Helen lived in a villa named Tivoli.

In Haiti, Frederick's main mission was to convince its dictator, General Louis Mondestin Florvil Hyppolite, to allow the U.S. Navy to have a base in Haiti's port town of Môle Saint-Nicolas.

Frederick was glad to be in Haiti, but the going was tough. He suffered from the heat at times. In that letter to Rosetta he said it was brutal. Still, he had ridden ten miles on horseback the previous day.

He was also having a difficult time with French. "I am making progress but I am yet far behind and almost despair." *Almost* being the operative word. He was determined to keep at it. "My motto is toil and trust."

At age seventy-two, Frederick couldn't toil as hard as he once had. There was trouble with his eyesight along with his energy. And worries: several friends and family members were ill, including Rosetta's oldest, Hattie. Then in February Helen came down with rheumatic fever and wasn't out of danger until late March. But toil on he did as best he could.

"Still I keep on my legs and at work with my brain and pen as usual," he wrote granddaughter Fredericka in February 1891. One of his projects was putting together a collection of his speeches, so that, "when I shall fall like a faded leaf from a living tree, somebody will once in a while study my words and works."

He also told Fredericka that he had recently heard from her cousin Joe and how happy he was to know that the young man was still working hard on his violin skills. "I almost ache to hear you say that you find time to do the same. You have talent and have ability." That said, he didn't want his granddaughter to neglect her studies. A young black woman would have enough to "contend with in the battle of life without having her hands tied as mine have been by a want of education."

Page one of Frederick's February 1891 letter to granddaughter Fredericka.

Twenty-year-old Fredericka (Rosetta's fifth born) was attending the Mechanics Institute in Rochester, New York. Her nineteen-year-old cousin Joe (Charley's second born) was on his way to being hailed a "genius on the violin."

Four months after that letter to Fredericka, Frederick resigned his post as minister resident to Haiti. Its government had refused to allow a U.S. naval base in its country. Give the Americans an inch and they'll take an ell—that was the fear. Part of Frederick was happy to see Haiti so protective of its autonomy.

Frederick was not happy about the production of the revised edition of *Life and Times,* to which he had added another hundred pages in bringing his life up-to-date. The paper was cheap, the binding sloppy. And this book was no bestseller. But when it came out in late 1892, Frederick had experienced something far more wounding than a lousy publisher. That summer Frederick Jr., age fifty and employed by the Pension Bureau, died in his home in Hillsdale, a neighborhood in Anacostia.

By then Frederick had attended many funerals, sent dozens of condolences. Several of his twenty-one grandchildren had died as babies, toddlers, and teens. Frederick Jr.'s wife, Virginia, had died while Frederick was in Haiti. So many of

Cabinet card, May 10, 1894: Frederick is with grandson Joseph Henry Douglass, who became a celebrated concert violinist. Between spring 1888 and early winter 1890 Joseph studied violin at the New England Conservatory for five semesters. He reportedly also studied at the Boston Conservatory.

the people he had fought with and against were also gone: Dr. James McCune Smith had died in 1865, Isaac Post in 1872, Charles Remond in 1873, Gerrit Smith, William Nell, and Charles Sumner in 1874, William Lloyd Garrison and John Jones in 1879, Lucretia Mott in 1880, Henry Highland Garnet in 1882, Sojourner Truth in 1883, Wendell Phillips in 1884, Martin Delany in 1885, Amy Post in 1889, and James Redpath in 1891. Now in July 1892 Frederick had lost a son.

On the old lion lived. Teas. Dinners. Speaking engagements. Invitations to dedicate schools and other institutions. The correspondence he received kept him plenty busy, too. Letters from old friends, such as Elizabeth Cady Stanton. Letters from new friends, such as the spitfire Ida B. Wells, journalist and anti-lynching crusader. Frederick also received letters from strangers. A librarian in Van Buren, Arkansas, asked for a photograph of him to hang on the walls of his library named in his honor. A professor wrote of a young artist who longed to do a life-size painting of Frederick.

Of course letters received meant letters to send, which Frederick sometimes fell behind on. In one dated February 4, 1894, he apologized to a friend for his delayed response. "I have been of late much afflicted with weakness of vision—unable to use my eyes but for brief periods," he explained. Frederick also had a bad case of "la grippe" (influenza). And he was tired. Back in 1893 he had served as commissioner of Haiti's pavilion at the World's Fair celebrating the 400th anniversary of Christopher Columbus' "discovery" of the New World. Held in Chicago, the fair was dedicated in October 1892 but didn't get under way until early 1893. The event, which was silent on the contributions of black Americans, had

Ida B. Wells (albumen print, c. 1893). Frederick applauded Wells for her anti-lynching crusade and adored her for her graciousness toward Helen when many black women gave her the cold shoulder. He wrote the introduction to Wells' pamphlet *The Reason Why the Colored American Is Not in the World's Columbian Exposition.*

Frederick and Helen living in Chicago for months. "I had much talking to do during those eight months and at times I felt that my time had come to ask for a rest," said Frederick in that February 4, 1894, letter.

A year later, Wednesday, February 20, 1895, was hardly a day of rest for Frederick, who had recently turned seventy-seven

Frederick Douglass in His Study at Cedar Hill (albumen print, c. 1893). Frederick is surrounded by more than two thousand books. They include the copy of the *Columbian Orator* he purchased as a boy. On the rolltop desk sits his violin. One of the items on the wall to Frederick's left is a photograph of himself. On the floor to his right (and very hard to see) is his English mastiff, Frank. This is the only known photograph of Frederick with his back to the camera.

and had a summer home under construction in Maryland, overlooking the Chesapeake Bay. He spent most of that Wednesday at a meeting on women's suffrage in the capital. That night he had a speaking engagement at Hillsdale African Church near his home. He and Helen, having supped, were standing in Cedar Hill's front hall waiting for a carriage to take them to Hillsdale when Frederick, after being quite animated, suddenly

He was the grandest man of African descent this century has seen.

—THE RECORDER
of Norfolk, Virginia

We do not expect to see another [Frederick] Douglass.

—THE SUN
of Providence, Rhode Island

collapsed and he—reader, teacher, orator, self-emancipator, abolitionist, author, editor, publisher, intellectual, civil rights activist, women's rights activist, public servant, diplomat, statesman, humanitarian, husband, father, grandfather— Frederick, like a faded leaf, fell from a living tree.

As he once wrote of Abraham Lincoln's passing, "a hush fell upon the land."

Cabinet card, October 31, 1894: This photograph was taken four months before Frederick died in New Bedford, Massachusetts, where he began his life in freedom.

The whole history of the progress of human liberty shows that all concessions yet made to her august claims have been born of earnest struggle . . . . If there is no struggle there is no progress. Those who profess to favor freedom and yet deprecate agitation are men who want crops without plowing up the ground, they want rain without thunder and lightning. They want the ocean without the awful roar of its many waters.

This struggle may be a moral one, or it may be a physical one, and it may be both moral and physical, but it must be a struggle. Power concedes nothing without a demand. It never did and it never will. Find out just what any people will quietly submit to and you have found the exact measure of injustice and wrong which will be imposed upon them, and these will continue till they are resisted with either words or blows, or with both. The limits of tyrants are prescribed by the endurance of those whom they oppress . . . . Men may not get all they pay for in this world, but they must certainly pay for all they get. If we ever get free from the oppressions and wrongs heaped upon us, we must pay for their removal. We must do this by labor, by suffering, by sacrifice, and if needs be, by our lives and the lives of others.

—**FREDERICK DOUGLASS**, August 3, 1857

169

Author's Note

SEVERAL YEARS AGO I HAD THE HONOR of delivering the keynote address for the Annual Community Meeting of the Frederick Douglass Memorial and Historical Association in Washington, D.C. Before the program a National Park Service ranger treated me to a private tour of Frederick's final home, Cedar Hill.

Knowing about Frederick's life and times is one thing, but to move about his home—see his desk and spectacles, his violin, the family's sitting room, the parlor for guests, the room in which he slept—that was an experience like no other.

By the time I visited Cedar Hill, Frederick Douglass had appeared in several of my books; he would appear in future ones. As I wrote him into *Maritcha, Cause: Reconstruction America, Emancipation Proclamation,* and *Capital Days,* as I quick-sketched him in *Portraits of African-American Heroes,* I always felt a tug, a soft longing to do a book on him. I wanted to get to know better this man who, as Elizabeth Cady Stanton so rightly said, was "majestic in his wrath," this man who, as poet Robert Hayden put it, was "superb in love and logic." I yearned to know in my heart, not just in my head, why so many schools, parks, bridges, streets, centers, housing developments, neighborhoods, associations bear his name. Why so many statues and monuments?

1 Frederick's inkstand is set off by a stag's antlers to hold his pen.

2 Frederick's top hat.

3 A stereoscope with a stereo view card in place. Stereo view cards present a left- and right-eye view of the same image. When seen through the stereoscope, the image appears to be 3-D.

These are just a few of the hundreds of artifacts from Frederick's life to be found at Cedar Hill. Declared a national historic building by Congress in 1962, Cedar Hill underwent extensive restoration. It opened to the public as the Frederick Douglass National Historic Site ten years later, on February 14, Frederick's adopted birthday.

Also during school visits when the name Frederick Douglass came up, I have often been saddened by young people's responses as to who he was. Most had little more to say than that he was an "escaped slave," an abolitionist, and a great speaker.

"Escaped slave?"

Frederick, who lived for seventy-seven years, spent about a quarter of his life in slavery. But why refer to someone who regained his liberty as an "escaped slave" as if "slave" was his everlasting identity as opposed to his legal status for a time?

As William S. McFeely pointed out in his biography *Frederick Douglass*, Frederick once told his colleague James Redpath, "I shall never get beyond Frederick Douglass the self-educated fugitive slave." McFeely went on to say, "And indeed the American public never let him escape from being thought of as a runaway slave. Most white people could not see him as other than that remarkable colored fellow; in this Douglass shared an experience that every black intellectual in America has faced."

It is my hope that *Facing Frederick* will inspire readers to take a good long look at, and think more deeply about, a multifaceted, monumental man. A man utterly beyond category.

Frederick facing left in a
c. 1850 daguerreotype.

"Frederick Douglass"

BY ROBERT HAYDEN

When it is finally ours, this freedom, this liberty, this beautiful

and terrible thing, needful to man as air,

usable as earth; when it belongs at last to all,

when it is truly instinct, brain matter, diastole, systole,

reflex action; when it is finally won; when it is more

than the gaudy mumbo jumbo of politicians:

this man, this Douglass, this former slave, this Negro

beaten to his knees, exiled, visioning a world

where none is lonely, none hunted, alien,

this man, superb in love and logic, this man

shall be remembered. Oh, not with statues' rhetoric,

not with legends and poems and wreaths of bronze alone,

but with the lives grown out of his life, the lives

fleshing his dream of the beautiful, needful thing.

Time Line

FEBRUARY 1818 Born Frederick Augustus Washington Bailey to Harriet Bailey on Aaron Anthony's Holme Hill Farm on Maryland's Eastern Shore. Aaron Anthony, his mother's owner and possibly his father, is the overseer of Edward Lloyd's property, which includes thirteen plantations worked by more than five hundred enslaved people.

1818–1823 Raised on Holme Hill Farm by grandmother Betsey Bailey, also owned by Aaron Anthony and married to a free man, Isaac Bailey, a sawyer.

1820 Sister Kitty is born.

1822 Sister Arianna is born.

AUGUST 1824 Taken to live in Aaron Anthony's home on Lloyd's Wye River plantation. Also living there are his older siblings Perry (born 1813), Sarah (born 1814),
and Eliza (born 1816).

FEBRUARY 1825 Sees his mother for the last time.

LATE 1825 OR EARLY 1826 Mother dies.

MARCH 1826 Sent to Baltimore to serve ship's carpenter Hugh Auld; his wife,
Sophie; and their son, Thomas. The Aulds live in the Fells Point section of Balti-
more. Hugh Auld's brother, Thomas, is married to Lucretia Anthony, daughter of
Aaron Anthony, still Frederick's owner.

NOVEMBER 14, 1826 Aaron Anthony dies and Frederick continues to serve Hugh
Auld in Baltimore.

JULY 6, 1827 Lucretia Auld, who had inherited Frederick, dies and he becomes the
property of her husband, Thomas Auld, but he continues to serve Thomas' brother,
Hugh.

1828–1830 Hired out to work in a Baltimore shipyard.

1831–1832 Joins Bethel AME Church, mentored by Charles Lawson, and buys a copy
of *The Columbian Orator*.

MARCH 1833 Sent to Thomas Auld in St. Michaels, Maryland.

JANUARY 1, 1834 Because of his rebelliousness, rented out to slave breaker Edward
Covey.

JANUARY 1, 1835 Rented out to farmer William Freeland.

APRIL 2, 1836 Authorities learn of his plot to escape.

APRIL 1836 Returned to Baltimore to learn to be a caulker. While there he meets
Anna Murray.

SEPTEMBER 3, 1838 Escapes from Baltimore and arrives in New York City the next
day as Frederick Johnson.

SEPTEMBER 15, 1838 Married to Anna by the Reverend J. W. C. Pennington, who
escaped slavery in Maryland in 1827.

SEPTEMBER 17, 1838 Heads to New Bedford, Massachusetts, with Anna, where
they stay briefly with a black couple, Nathan and Polly Johnson, who own a catering
business and a confectionery shop. While with them, Mr. Johnson suggests that

Frederick change his surname from Johnson because there are a lot of Johnsons in New Bedford. Frederick is soon known as Frederick Douglass. When Frederick and Anna leave the Johnsons, they move into a small place at 157 Elm Street. They later move into a larger house at 111 Ray Street (now Acushnet Avenue).

JUNE 24, 1839 First child, daughter Rosetta, is born.

OCTOBER 9, 1840 Son Lewis Henry is born.

AUGUST 10–12, 1841 Attends MASS convention in Nantucket, during which he delivers a speech that launches his career as a lecturer.

FALL 1841 Moves to Lynn, Massachusetts.

MARCH 3, 1842 Second son, Frederick Jr., is born.

AUGUST 15–19, 1843 Attends national convention of black men in Buffalo, New York, during which he clashes with Henry Highland Garnet over his "Address to the Slaves" (also known as "Call to Rebellion"), in which Garnet urged enslaved people to liberate themselves by any means necessary, insinuating even by bloody revolt. Frederick successfully leads the charge against the convention's endorsing Garnet's address.

SEPTEMBER 16, 1843 Physically assaulted by a proslavery mob in Pendleton, Indiana.

OCTOBER 21, 1844 Third son, Charles Remond, is born.

MAY 23, 1845 Publication of first autobiography, *Narrative of the Life of Frederick Douglass*.

AUGUST 16, 1845 Leaves to lecture in the British Isles.

AUGUST 27, 1845 During his voyage to England aboard the British ship *Cambria,* the captain asks him to give a lecture. When he attempts to do so, he has to face down a crowd of proslavery American passengers who call him a liar and threaten to throw him overboard. Denied a cabin because he was black, Frederick was forced to bunk in steerage during the twelve-day journey.

AUGUST 28, 1845 Arrives in Liverpool, England.

SEPTEMBER 1845 Publication of first Dublin edition of *Narrative*.

OCTOBER 25, 1845 Thomas Auld transfers ownership of him to his brother, Hugh, for $100.

OCTOBER 6, 1846 Hugh Auld sells Frederick's freedom to British supporters for £150 sterling ($711.66 in American currency).

DECEMBER 12, 1846 Officially free when manumission papers are filed in Baltimore County court.

APRIL 4, 1847 Boards the *Cambria* in Liverpool and begins journey home.

APRIL 20, 1847 Arrives in Boston.

DECEMBER 3, 1847 Debut of his first newspaper, the *North Star*.

FEBRUARY 1848 Moves family to Rochester.

JULY 19–20, 1848 Attends women's rights convention in Seneca Falls, New York.

MARCH 22, 1849 Second daughter, Annie, is born.

MAY 5, 1849 Physically assaulted by a group of white men while walking along the Battery in New York City with two white British friends, Julia and Eliza Griffiths.

MAY 9, 1851 Publicly breaks with Garrison.

JUNE 26, 1851 Debut of second newspaper, *Frederick Douglass' Paper*.

JULY 5, 1852 In Rochester's Corinthian Hall delivers one of his best-known speeches, "The Meaning of July Fourth to the Negro" (often referred to as "What to the Slave is the Fourth of July?").

1853 Publication in Julia Griffiths' anthology, *Autographs for Freedom*, and in his newspaper of his novella *The Heroic Slave*, based on the successful 1841 slave revolt Madison Washington led aboard the slave ship *Creole* heading from Virginia to New Orleans. *The Heroic Slave* is Frederick's only work of fiction and one of the first known works of fiction by a black person in the United States.

JUNE 26–28, 1855 Attends a convention in Syracuse, New York, where he helps form the Radical Abolition Party, which advocates land redistribution, voting rights for all, and the abolition of slavery by any means necessary, including violence. Cofounders include Gerrit Smith, John Brown, and Dr. James McCune Smith.

AUGUST 1855 Publication of second autobiography, *My Bondage and My Freedom,* which will sell 15,000 copies in two months.

JUNE 1858 Debut of *Douglass' Monthly*.

OCTOBER 17, 1859 While delivering for the first time his speech "Self-Made Men" in Philadelphia, learns of the failure of John Brown's raid in Harpers Ferry and that the authorities are on the hunt for him as a co-conspirator.

NOVEMBER 12, 1859 Sails from Quebec to England.

MARCH 13, 1860 Daughter Annie dies; he hurries home after being notified of the loss.

DECEMBER 3, 1860 Along with other abolitionists, Frederick is physically attacked by a proslavery mob in Boston's Tremont Temple during a commemoration of the first anniversary of John Brown's execution.

APRIL 1861 Welcomes the outbreak of the Civil War.

JANUARY 1, 1863 Celebrates with other abolitionists in Boston's Tremont Temple Lincoln's signing of the Emancipation Proclamation.

FEBRUARY 24, 1863 Becomes a recruiter for the Union Army.

AUGUST 10, 1863 Goes to D.C. to speak with President Lincoln about the discrimination black troops face. Also meets with Secretary of War Stanton, leaving with the expectation that he will be made a commissioned officer.

AUGUST 16, 1863 Ceases publication of his third newspaper, *Douglass' Monthly*.

NOVEMBER 17, 1864 Goes to Maryland for the first time since his escape twenty-six years earlier, and reunites with his sister Eliza.

MARCH 4, 1865 Attends Lincoln's second inauguration and the ball that follows.

MAY 9–10, 1865 Attends the American Anti-Slavery Society's thirty-second annual meeting in New York, where he sides with members who do not think the organization should be dissolved.

FEBRUARY 1867 Receives a letter from his brother, Perry, whom he has not seen in forty years.

JULY 1867 Brother Perry arrives in Rochester with his wife and four children.

LATE SUMMER–FALL 1868 Campaigns for General Ulysses S. Grant for president.

MAY 19, 1870 Is one of the honored guests at a grand parade celebrating the Fifteenth Amendment in Baltimore, where he addresses a crowd of 10,000.

SUMMER 1870 Buys half interest in failing *New Era* for $8,000, becomes its editor in chief, and changes its name to *New National Era*.

LATE 1870 Buys remaining half interest in *New National Era*.

JANUARY 12, 1871 Appointed by President Grant assistant secretary of a commission of inquiry looking into annexation of the Dominican Republic (then Santo Domingo), which never happens.

MAY 11–12, 1872 Nominated by Equal Rights Party to be running mate of white reformer Victoria Woodhull in her bid for the presidency. He doesn't accept the nomination.

JUNE 2, 1872 Rochester home burns to the ground possibly because of an act of arson.

JULY 1872 Moves family to Washington, D.C., and into a house on Capitol Hill.

MARCH 10, 1873 Gives details on his escape from slavery for the first time in a lecture in Philadelphia.

APRIL 1873 Turns *New National Era* over to sons Lewis and Frederick Jr.

MARCH 14, 1874 Made president of the Freedman's Bank.

OCTOBER 22, 1874 Last issue of the *New National Era*.

APRIL 14, 1876 Keynote speaker at the unveiling of a monument to Lincoln, the Freedmen's Memorial, in Washington, D.C.'s Lincoln Park.

MARCH 17, 1877 U.S. Senate confirms his appointment as D.C.'s marshal, making him the first black American whose presidential appointment required Senate approval.

JUNE 17, 1877 Visits St. Michaels, Maryland, and meets with former owner Thomas Auld, now in his eighties.

SEPTEMBER 1, 1877 Buys a nearly ten-acre estate in present-day Anacostia for $6,700 and names it Cedar Hill. He later buys adjacent land.

JUNE 2, 1879 Delivers the main eulogy at a memorial service in Washington, D.C., for William Lloyd Garrison.

JANUARY 1881 Publication of third autobiography, *Life and Times of Frederick Douglass,* which has abysmal sales.

MARCH 1881 Appointed D.C.'s recorder of deeds by President Garfield.

AUGUST 4, 1882 Wife, Anna, dies.

JANUARY 24, 1884 Marries Helen Pitts.

JANUARY 5, 1886 Resigns as D.C.'s recorder of deeds at President Grover Cleveland's request.

SEPTEMBER 15, 1886 With Helen sails to England, the start of a long vacation that will take them to many European nations and to Egypt.

SUMMER 1887 Returns to the States.

JULY 1, 1889 Made minister resident and consul general to Haiti by President Benjamin Harrison.

SEPTEMBER 1889 Made chargé d'affaires for the Dominican Republic.

JULY 30, 1891 Resigns as minister resident and consul general to Haiti.

JULY 26, 1892 Frederick Jr. dies.

DECEMBER 1892 A revised edition of *Life and Times of Frederick Douglass* is published.

1892–1893 Serves as commissioner of Haiti's exhibit at World's Fair in Chicago.

JANUARY 9, 1894 Delivers the speech "Lessons of the Hour" at Washington's Metropolitan AME Church. This more than 14,000-word stinging indictment of the widespread lynching of black Americans is his last major speech and one of his greatest.

1894–1895 Construction of Twin Oaks, his summer home overlooking the Chesapeake Bay in the black resort town of Highland Beach, Maryland, developed by son Charley, whose youngest son, Haley George Douglass, will one day be its mayor. Frederick dies before his summer home is completed.

FEBRUARY 20, 1895 Dies at Cedar Hill at the age of seventy-seven after spending much of the day at a meeting of the National Council of Women and shortly before he is to speak at Hillsdale African Church near his home.

FEBRUARY 25, 1895 Family funeral services held at Cedar Hill, followed by a memorial service in a packed Metropolitan AME Church. Distinguished guests include Susan B. Anthony, Justice John Harlan, and black politicians Blanche K. Bruce and P. B. S. Pinchback. Flower arrangements are too numerous to count. One is from Benjamin Franklin Auld, son of Frederick's last owner, Hugh Auld.

FEBRUARY 26, 1895 Body lies in state in Rochester City Hall, followed by funeral services at Rochester Central Presbyterian Church, then burial in the city's Mount Hope Cemetery beside his first wife, Anna, and their second daughter, Annie.

Notes

OR THE SAKE OF CLARITY, I HAVE MODERN-
ized some punctuation and spelling. For complete citations for books heavily consulted, please see Selected Sources.

EPIGRAPH

iii "Frederick Douglass was in love with photography": John Stauffer et al., *Picturing Frederick Douglass*, p. ix.

A NOTE ON EARLY PHOTOGRAPHY

vi "a deep-seated want" and "see themselves as others": Frederick Douglass, "Pictures and Progress," in Stauffer et al., *Picturing Frederick Douglass*, p. 165.

vi "the great discoverer of modern times": Douglass, "Pictures and Progress," in Stauffer, et al., *Picturing Frederick Douglass*, p. 164.

❶ A SOUL TO ASPIRE

1 "sacred cause": Douglass, *Narrative of the Life of Frederick Douglass*, p. 125.

3 "my meat and my drink": Douglass, *Narrative*, p. 117.

5 "I felt myself a slave": Douglass, *Narrative*, p. 117.

5 the call-and-response: Parker Pillsbury, *Acts of the Anti-Slavery Apostles* (Concord, New Hampshire: n.p., 1883), p. 328.

6 "This is an extraordinary man": in James M. Gregory, *Frederick Douglass the Orator* (Springfield, Massachusetts: Willey & Co., 1893), p. 99.

8 "He was more than six feet": David N. Johnson, *Sketches of Lynn, or the Changes of Fifty Years* (Lynn: Thos. P. Nichols, printer, 1880), p. 230.

8 "*in their proper place . . . don't know more*": Douglass, "The Church and Prejudice," in Philip S. Foner and Yuval Taylor, eds., *Frederick Douglass: Selected Speeches and Writings*.

9 "twin-monsters of darkness": Douglass, "The Folly of Our Opponents," in Foner and Taylor, *Frederick Douglass*.

9 Frederick's early earnings in New Bedford: William S. McFeely, *Frederick Douglass*, pp. 79–80.

11 "emmeadiately . . . worte": Douglass to Abigail Kelley, Richard Dowden Richard, and Richard D. Webb, in John R. McKivigan, ed., *The Frederick Douglass Papers, Series Three: Correspondence, Volume 1, 1842–1852,* pp. 8, 66, 71.

11 "I was born in Tuckahoe": Douglass, *Narrative*, p. 1.

11 "the hope of being free": Douglass, *Narrative*, p. 41.

12 "with saddened heart . . . to the mighty ocean": Douglass, *Narrative*, p. 64.

13 "beck and call" and "Kill him! Kill him!": Douglass, *Narrative*, pp. 94, 96.

13 "On the Starry Heavens," "The Dignity of Human Nature," and "Dialogue between a Master and Slave": Caleb Bingham, *The Columbian Orator* (Boston: np, 1817), pp. v–vi.

14 "unarmed mariner . . . man-of-war": Douglass, *Narrative*, p. 107.

❷ ONE THE WORLD OVER

18 "I hope we shall": "Letter from James Haughton—The League and American Slavery," *Liberator*, July 25, 1845, p. 119.

19 "It is the most thrilling work": *Lynn Pioneer* reprinted in *Liberator*, May 30, 1845, p. 86.

20 "I have wept over": A.M., "Narrative of Douglass," *Liberator*, June 6, 1845, p. 89.

21 "Frederick Douglass, the Fugitive Slave": *Massachusetts Spy*, August 27, 1845, p. 4.

24 "We are highly gratified": "From the *Cork Examiner*," *Liberator*, November 28, 1845, p. 189.

26 "almost literally alive with beggars . . . for his anti-slavery faith": Douglass to William Lloyd Garrison, February 26, 1846, in McKivigan, *Frederick Douglass Papers*, pp. 95–96.

26 "fits of melancholy . . . at times": Douglass to Ruth Cox (aka Harriet Bailey), May 16, 1846, in McKivigan, *Douglass Papers*, p. 125.

27 "robbery of Mexico": Douglass to William A. White, July 30, 1846, in McKivigan, *Frederick Douglass Papers*, p. 148.

27–28 "Well, all my books . . . I want more": Douglass to Richard D. Webb, December 6, 1845, in McKivigan, *Frederick Douglass Papers*, pp. 69–70.

29 "Get as good": Douglass to Richard D. Webb, mid-January 1846, in McKivigan, ed., *Frederick Douglass Papers*, p. 80.

30 money earned on first Dublin edition of *Narrative*: Robert S. Levine, "Taking Back the *Narrative*: The Dublin Editions," in *The Lives of Frederick Douglass*.

31 "We will take care of the philosophy": Douglass, *My Bondage and My Freedom*, p. 361.

31 "Hereditary bondsmen! . . . strike the blow?": Lord Byron, *Childe Harold's Pilgrimage: A Romaunt*, Canto II, stanza LXXV (London: printed for John Murray, 32, Fleet-street; William Blackwood, Edinburgh; and John Cumming, Dublin. By Thomas Davison, White-Friars, 1812), p. 102.

32 "No Union with Slaveholders": *Liberator*, January 3, 1845, 1 (on masthead).

32 Letter to Pease: Douglass to Elizabeth Pease, July 6, 1846, in McKivigan, ed., *Frederick Douglass Papers*, p. 142.

32–33 "covenant with death . . . hell": Henry Mayer, *All on Fire: William Lloyd Garrison and the Abolition of Slavery* (St. Martin's Press, 1998), p. 531.

33 "I was growing, and needed room": Douglass, *My Bondage*, p. 362.

34 "I trust I need . . . wrongs and horrors": *Report of Proceedings at the Soirée Given to Frederick Douglass, London Tavern, March 30, 1847* (London: R. Yorke Clarke and Co., 1847), p. 3.

35 "the free upgushings of . . . the present moment": "Farewell Speech of Mr. Frederick Douglass Previously to Embarking on Board the *Cambria* upon His Return to America, Delivered at the Valedictory Soiree Given to Him at the London Tavern on March 30, 1847, London, 1847," rbscp.lib.rochester.edu/4395.

❸ SHIPS UPON A STORMY SEA

37 "running and dancing": Douglass to Anna Richardson, April 29, 1847, in McKivigan, *Frederick Douglass Papers*, p. 208.

39 "smooth the tucks . . . made it so": Rosetta Douglass Sprague, "Anna Murray

Douglass—My Mother as I Recall Her," *Journal of Negro History*, Vol. 8, No. 1, January 1923, p. 97.

41 "My dear Anna . . . seldom enjoys good health": Douglass to Anna Richardson, April 29, 1847, in McKivigan, *Frederick Douglass Papers*, p. 208.

41–42 Quincy on Frederick: McFeely, *Frederick Douglass*, p. 147.

42 earnings cap: McKivigan, *Frederick Douglass Papers*, pp. 226–27, note 2.

42 Frederick's activity during his tour: Douglass to Joseph Barker, October 16, 1847, in McKivigan, *Frederick Douglass Papers*, p. 264.

43 "an excellent and elegant [printing] press": Douglass to J. D. Carr, November 1, 1847, in McKivigan, *Frederick Douglass Papers,* pp. 266–67.

44 On Hunter and Moore being tenants in the Talman Building: *Daily American Directory of the City of Rochester* (Rochester: Jerome & Brother, 1847), pp. 137, 171.

44 "[Frederick] never opened to me": William Lloyd Garrison to Helen E. Garrison, October 20, 1847, in Walter M. Merrill, ed., *The Letters of William Lloyd Garrison, Volume 3: No Union with Slaveholders, 1841–1849* (Cambridge, MA: Belknap Press, 1974), p. 533.

44 *North Star* mission statement and motto: *North Star*, December 3, 1847, p. 1.

47 "The [first issue] of the *North Star*": David Ruggles to Frederick Douglass and Martin Delany, January 1, 1848, in McKivigan, *Frederick Douglass Papers*, p. 281.

47 David Peck's humiliation: "Massachusetts vs. Pennsylvania: Colorphobia in Pennsylvania," *North Star*, February 4, 1848, p. 3.

48 "I hasten to congratulate you": Samuel J. May to Frederick Douglass, December 9, 1847, in McKivigan, *Frederick Douglass Papers*, pp. 278–79.

49 "We regard [Frederick Douglass]": "Notices of the *North Star*," *North Star*, January 7, 1848, p. 3.

49 "We live in times . . . with the contest": "Frederick Douglass' Address," *North Star*, August 4, 1848, p. 2.

51 Jane Marsh Parker's remembrances and quotes: Jane Marsh Parker, "Reminiscences of Frederick Douglass," *The Outlook*, April 6, 1895, p. 552.

51   "not been well": Douglass to Abigail and Lydia Mott, February 21, 1848, in McKivigan, *Frederick Douglass Papers*, p. 297.

❹ THE VOICE OF INSPIRATION

53   "very foolishly": Douglass to Gerrit Smith, March 30, 1849, in McKivigan, *Frederick Douglass Papers*, p. 375.

54   cost of printing the *North Star*: McFeely, *Frederick Douglass*, p. 153.

54   "I fear I have miscalculated": Douglass to Julia Griffiths, April 28, 1848, in McKivigan, *Frederick Douglass Papers*, p. 302.

54   *North Star* expenses and number of subscribers: Will Fassett, Douglass, "*The North Star*, 1847–1849," rbscp.lib.rochester.edu/2524.

55   "a very encouraging list . . . drops of the coming shower!": John S. Mott, "To Our Friends," *North Star*, May 19, 1848, p. 2.

55   "Though I have suffered": *North Star*, June 30, 1848, p. 2.

55   "not more than two thousand": Douglass, "What Are the Colored People Doing for Themselves?" *North Star*, July 14, 1848, p. 2.

56   "the power to . . . be secured": Waldo E. Martin, *The Mind of Frederick Douglass* (University of North Carolina Press, 1986), p. 147.

57   "The speaking, addresses": "The Rights of Women," *North Star*, July 28, 1848, p. 3.

59–60 Frederick's keynote in Cleveland: "An Address to the Colored People of the United States," in Foner and Taylor, *Frederick Douglass*.

61   "I get along pretty well . . . because I am colored": Douglass to Horatio G. Warner, September 22, 1848, in McKivigan, *Frederick Douglass Papers*, p. 320.

61   "the pulse of my heart": Frederick Douglass probably to one of the Mott sisters, April 27, 1847. Frederick Douglass Papers at the Library of Congress. 1847. Manuscript/Mixed Material. Retrieved from the Library of Congress, www.loc.gov/item/mfd.03003, p. 1 (accessed June 25, 2016).

62   "degrade an innocent child": Douglass to Horatio G. Warner, September 22, 1848, in McKivigan, *Frederick Douglass Papers*, p. 322.

63   "Jezebel": "Frederick Douglass," *National Anti-Slavery Standard*, September 24, 1853, p. 70.

63   Griffiths on Frederick's health and "incapable of using": David W. Blight, *Frederick Douglass' Civil War*, pp. 20–21.

64   "great-hearted": Douglass, *Life and Times* (1892), p. 370.

65   "domestic tranquility . . . blessings of liberty": U.S. Constitution, Our Documents, www.ourdocuments.gov/doc.php?doc=9&page=transcript (accessed August 1, 2016).

❺ NO TIME FOR US TO LEAVE THE COUNTRY

69   "The paper must be clean . . . I will raise myself": Frederick Douglass to Gerrit Smith, June 4, 1851, in McKivigan, *Frederick Douglass Papers*, p. 451.

69   "In becoming a voter": "Position of Frederick Douglas," *Liberator*, July 4, 1851, p. 108.

70   "The *North Star* makes its appearance": "Frederick Douglass' Paper," *Liberator*, July 4, 1851, p. 107.

70   "his balance of mind . . . going crazy": Blight, *Frederick Douglass' Civil War*, p. 21.

72   "Amid all our afflictions": Douglass, "The Free Negro's Place in America," in Foner and Taylor, eds., *Frederick Douglass*.

72   "a hell-black enactment": Douglass, "The Meaning of July Fourth for the Negro," in Foner and Taylor, *Frederick Douglass*.

73   "called up at all hours": Rosetta Douglass Sprague, "Anna Murray Douglass— My Mother as I Recall Her," *Journal of Negro History*, vol. 8, no. 1, January 1923, p. 98.

73   "an attempt to bail out": Douglass, *Life and Times*, p. 329.

74   "I have wrought in the day": Douglass to Harriet Tubman, August 29, 1868, Sarah Hopkins Bradford, *Scenes in the Life of Harriet Tubman* (Auburn, New York: W.J. Moses, printer, 1869), p. 7.

75–76 "This Fourth [of] July is *yours* . . . 'Be driven'": Douglass, "The Meaning of July Fourth for the Negro," in Foner and Taylor, *Frederick Douglass*.

76 "The ten thousand horrors": Douglass, "The Claims of the Negro Ethnologically Considered," in Foner and Taylor, *Frederick Douglass.*

77 "life of prayer" and "a great work": Douglass, *My Bondage and My Freedom,* pp. 167–168.

77 "I am sober . . . will triumph": Douglass, *My Bondage and My Freedom,* pp. 461, 464.

77 "This morning is the third": "Unprecedented Sale," *Auburn Daily Advertiser* reprinted in *Frederick Douglass' Paper,* August 24, 1855, p. 2.

78 "so far inferior": Paul Finkelman, *Dred Scott v. Sandford: A Brief History with Documents* (Boston: Bedford-St. Martin's, 1997), p. 61.

79 "You will readily ask . . . the Almighty is greater": Douglass, "The Dred Scott Decision," in Foner and Taylor, *Frederick Douglass.*

79 "upon the lying assumption": "African Civilization Society," *Douglass' Monthly,* February 1859, p. 19.

80 Frederick's attempt to sabotage Garnet's trip to England: "Rev. Henry Highland Garnet," *North Star,* July 27, 1849, p. 2.

81 "I thank God": Douglass, Robert S. Levine, *Martin Delany, Frederick Douglass, and the Politics of Representative Identity.*

81 "I knew, sir, that in your hot pursuit": Henry Highland Garnet, "'Calling Him Out,' and He Comes," *North Star,* September 7, 1849, p. 2.

82 "lean, strong . . . light and fire": Douglass, *Life and Times,* p. 339.

82 "Come with me": Douglass, *Life and Times,* p. 390.

84 "ferreting out and bringing to punishment": Douglass, *Life and Times,* p. 377.

85 "Tell Lewis . . . is still on the drawer": Douglass, *Life and Times,* p. 378.

85 "His zeal in the cause": Douglass, *John Brown: An Address at the Fourteenth Anniversary of Storer College, Harpers Ferry Virginia, May 30, 1881* (Dover, NH: Morning Star Job Printing House, 1881), p. 9.

86 "the light and life": Douglass, *Life and Times,* p. 394.

86 "We shall speak to you *weekly*": Douglass, "A Word of Explanation," *Douglass' Monthly,* August 1860, p. 305.

87 "Open thy mouth": *Douglass' Monthly,* August 1860, p. 305.

87   "The future of the anti-slavery cause": Douglass, "The Prospect in the Future," *Douglass' Monthly*, August 1860, p. 306.

89   "wisdom and virtue . . . upon her guilty head": Douglass, "The Union and How to Save It," *Douglass' Monthly*, February 1861, p. 402.

91   "This is no time for us to leave the country": Douglass, "A Trip to Hayti," *Douglass' Monthly*, May 1, 1861, p. 450.

❻ WE ARE ALL LIBERATED

95   "The national edifice . . . rules the hour": Douglass, "Fighting Rebels with Only One Hand," *Douglass' Monthly*, September 1861, p. 516.

95   "The same cruel prejudice": "The Star-Spangled Banner and the Duty of Colored Americans to that Flag," *Christian Recorder*, April 27, 1861, p. 62.

96   "from tallow and fat fried from dead Yankees": Douglass, "Signs of Barbarism," *Douglass' Monthly*, December 1861, p. 567.

96   "its root and its sap . . . drinking vessels" and on bones for drumsticks: Douglass, "The Slaveholders' Rebellion," *Douglass' Monthly*, August 1862, p. 689.

96   "DEAR SIR:—In your last issue": S. Dutton, "Signs of the Times," *Douglass' Monthly*, November 1, 1861, p. 547.

97   "Our government is taking": Douglass, "Position of the Government Toward Slavery," *Douglass' Monthly*, June 1861, p. 466.

97   "I trust I am not dreaming": Blight, *Frederick Douglass' Civil War*, p. 108.

98   "At last there is some ground of hope": "The Confiscation and Emancipation Law," *Douglass' Monthly*, August 1862, p. 695.

98   "We are all liberated . . . the black man is liberated": "Frederick Douglass at the Cooper Institute: The Proclamation and a Negro Army," *Douglass' Monthly*, March 1863, p. 805.

99   "A very large audience": "Frederick Douglass at the Cooper Institute," *New-York Daily Tribune*, February 7, 1863, p. 8.

101 "They said that it was known": "The Effects of the Proclamation—Freed Negroes Coming into Our Lines at Newbern, North Carolina," *Harper's Weekly*, February 21, 1863, p. 119.

103 "The grape and canister. . . made to come up": Lewis Douglass, "From Charleston," *Douglass' Monthly*, August 1863, p. 852.

103 "The day dawns": Douglass, "Men of Color, to Arms!" *Douglass' Monthly*, March 1863, p. 801.

107–108 "The calamity . . . that few could at first believe it": Frederick Douglass, "Abraham Lincoln, a Speech." Manuscript/Mixed Material. Retrieved from the Library of Congress, www.loc.gov/item/mfd.22015, p. 2 (accessed May 26, 2016).

109 "Neither slavery nor involuntary servitude": Thirteenth Amendment, Our Documents, www.ourdocuments.gov/doc.php?doc=40&page=transcript.

❼ A NEW WORLD

111–112 "Slavery is not abolished until," "a delusion, a mockery," and "Where shall the black man look": Douglass, "The Need for Continuing Anti-Slavery Work," in Foner and Taylor, *Frederick Douglass*.

112 "knows enough to pay taxes": "What the Black Man Wants," William D. Kelley, *The Equality of all Men Before the Law Claimed and Defended*. (Boston: Geo. C. Rand & Avery, 1865), p. 38.

113 "This is a country for white men ": Tonya Bolden, *Cause*, p. 21.

115–116 "dismal as is the hour," "incapacity," and "They gave us the bullet": Douglass, "Douglass Institute," in Foner and Taylor, *Frederick Douglass*.

117 "You enfranchise your enemies": Douglass, "Interview with a Colored Delegation Respecting Suffrage," in Edward McPherson, *A Political Manual for 1866* (Washington, D.C.: Philp & Solomons, 1866), p. 55.

118 "It would be hard to surpass": "Our 'Poor White' President," *National Anti-Slavery Standard*, February 17, 1866 (second page in an issue without page numbers).

119 "President Johnson's well-known courtesy": Kappa, "Our Washington Letter," *Richmond Examiner*, February 9, 1866, p. 1.

119 "All persons born": Fourteenth Amendment, Our Documents, www.ourdocuments.gov/doc.php?doc=43&page=transcriptgov.

121 "on account of race": Fifteenth Amendment, Our Documents, www.ourdocuments.gov/doc.php?doc=44&page=transcript.

122 "Think of Patrick and Sambo": Elizabeth Cady Stanton, "Manhood Suffrage," *The Revolution*, December 24, 1868, p. 392.

122–124 "With us, the [suffrage] matter. . . because she is black": Elizabeth Cady Stanton, Susan B. Anthony, and Matilda Joslyn Gage, eds., *History of Woman Suffrage*, Vol. 2 (Rochester, New York: Charles Mann, 1887), p. 382.

124 Freedmen's Bureau reports of violence: Bolden, *Cause*, pp. 40–42.

125 "Henceforth we live . . . has a future": Douglass, "At Last, At Last, the Black Man Has a Future," *The Frederick Douglass Papers: Series 1: Speeches, Debates, and Interviews, Volume 4, 1864–80* (New Haven: Yale University Press, 1979), p. 266, accessed on the website of the Institute for American Thought of Indiana University, frederickdouglass.infoset.io/islandora/object/islandora%3A2811#page/1/mode/1up.

❽ PROMISES IN YOUR CONSTITUTION

128 "well-preserved mental and moral faculties": "Personal," *New National Era*, September 8, 1870, p. 2.

130 On Frederick's earnings: Gregory, *Frederick Douglass the Orator*, p. 54; Gates Jr., *Frederick Douglass: Autobiographies*. New York: Library of America, 1994, p. 1063; and Frederick Douglass Papers at the Library of Congress. Speaking Engagements and Fees Charged. 1872. Manuscript/mixed material. Retrieved from the Library of Congress, www.loc.gov/item/mfd.44008 (accessed May 31, 2017).

134 "Scarcely a trace" and "much damaged": "Letter from the Editor," *New National Era*, June 13, 1872, p. 2.

134 "scorched and charred beyond recovery": Victoria Sandwick Schmitt, "Rochester's Frederick Douglass," Part Two, *Rochester History*, Fall 2005, p. 17.

135 Frederick's shopping: Douglass. *Clothing, 1873 to 1889*. 1889, 1873. Manuscript/Mixed Material. Retrieved from the Library of Congress, www.loc.gov/item/mfd.43001, pp. 1, 8, 14 (accessed August 2, 2016).

138 "flourish": Douglass, "To the Depositors of the Freedman's Savings and Trust Co.," *New National Era*, June 25, 1874, p. 2.

140 "You say you have . . . promises in your Constitution?": Douglass, "Speech of Mr. Douglass," in *Official Proceedings of the National Republican Conventions of 1868, 1872, 1876 and 1880* (Minneapolis, MN: Charles W. Johnson, 1903) p. 251.

142 "There is no man living": Harriet Jacobs, *1877, Jan.–Mar.* January 5, 1877. Manuscript/Mixed Material. Retrieved from the Library of Congress, www.loc.gov/item/mfd.04010, p. 46 (accessed June 25, 2016).

144 "We believe that the craze": Rumor, "Rumor Protests," *People's Advocate*, December 11, 1880, p. 1.

146 "I am glad to have a shelter for him": McFeely, *Frederick Douglass*, p. 297.

147–148 on subscriptions and charities: Frederick Douglass, Subscriptions, Folder 1 of 2. 1882. Manuscript/Mixed Material. Retrieved from the Library of Congress, www.loc.gov/item/mfd.44011, pp. 3, 7, 15, 17, 18, 21, 24, 25, 29 (accessed July 8, 2016).

150 comments on Frederick's second marriage: quoted in "Mr. Douglass' Marriage: Sentiments of the Colored Press," *New York Globe*, February 9, 1884, p. 2.

❾ LEAF FROM A LIVING TREE

152 "I am writing . . . did not kill me": Douglass to Rosetta Douglass Sprague, January 23, 1891, in Correspondence, 1891 to 1892. Manuscript/Mixed Material. Retrieved from the Library of Congress, www.loc.gov/item/mfd.48006, pp. 6–7 (accessed June 3, 2016).

152 "stand beneath": McFeely, *Frederick Douglass*, p. 347

154 Frederick's net worth: Gates, *Frederick Douglass: Autobiographies*, p. 1,073.

154–155 "At two o'clk, or thereabout . . . Leaning Tower": Douglass, Frederick Douglass Diary Tour of Europe and Africa. September 15, 1886. Manuscript/Mixed Material. Retrieved from the Library of Congress, www.loc.gov/item/mfd.01001, pp. 8, 10, 13, 18, 19 (accessed August 1, 2016).

155 "an ingeneering triumph . . . delight to the eye": Frederick Douglass, Frederick Douglass Diary Tour of Europe and Africa. September 15, 1886. Manuscript/

Mixed Material. Retrieved from the Library of Congress, www.loc.gov/item/mfd.01001, p. 31 (accessed August 1, 2016).

156 "We decided to extend our visit . . . out of the house of Bondage": Douglass, Frederick Douglass Diary Tour of Europe and Africa. September 15, 1886. Manuscript/Mixed Material. Retrieved from the Library of Congress, www.loc.gov/item/mfd.01001, p. 33 (accessed August 1, 2016).

156 "that I should be plowing . . . and cheerful": Douglass, Frederick Douglass Diary Tour of Europe and Africa. September 15, 1886. Manuscript/Mixed Material. Retrieved from the Library of Congress, www.loc.gov/item/mfd.01001, p. 35 (accessed August 1, 2016).

157 "Mr. Frederick Douglass has just returned": "Fred Douglass' Tour," *Kansas City Star*, June 29, 1887, p. 2.

158–159 "It has swept over the land . . . after-coming generations": Douglass, "Speech at the Civil Rights Mass-Meeting Held at Lincoln Hall, October 22, 1883," www.teachingamericanhistory.org/library/document/the-civil-rights-case.

159 "With the help of God . . . slandered people": Douglass, *Speech at a Surprise Party on Douglass' 71st Birthday*. 1889. Manuscript/Mixed Material. Retrieved from the Library of Congress, www.loc.gov/item/mfd.25002, p. 2 (accessed July 4, 2016).

160 "I am making . . . toil and trust": Douglass to Rosetta Douglass Sprague, January 23, 1891, in Frederick Douglass and Rosetta Douglass Sprague. Correspondence, 1891 to 1892. Manuscript/Mixed Material. Retrieved from the Library of Congress, www.loc.gov/item/mfd.48006, p. 4 (accessed June 3, 2016).

161 "Still I keep on my legs . . . by a want of education": Douglass to Fredericka Sprague, February 20, 1891, in Frederick Douglass and Rosetta Douglass Sprague. Correspondence, 1891 to 1892. Manuscript/Mixed Material. Retrieved from the Library of Congress, www.loc.gov/item/mfd.48006, pp. 14–16 (accessed June 3, 2016).

162 "genius on the violin": "Joseph H. Douglass," *Washington Bee*, January 18, 1896, p. 11.

164–165 "I have been of late . . . ask for a rest": Douglass, February 4, 1894.

Manuscript/Mixed Material. Retrieved from the Library of Congress, www.loc.gov/item/mfd.10005, pp. 23, 25 (accessed June 4, 2016).

167 Quotes from the *Recorder* and the *Sun*: James T. Haley, *Afro-American Encyclopaedia* (Nashville, TN: Haley and Florida, 1895), pp. 410, 409.

167 "a hush fell upon the land": Blight, *Frederick Douglass' Civil War*, p. 111.

169 "The whole history of the progress": Douglass, "The Significance of Emancipation in the West Indies," Canandaigua, New York, August 3, 1857, rbscp.lib.rochester.edu/4398.

AUTHOR'S NOTE

170 "majestic in his wrath": Elizabeth Cady Stanton in Theodore Stanton and Harriot Stanton Blatch, eds. *Elizabeth Cady Stanton as Revealed in Her Letters, Diary and Reminiscences*, vol. 2 (New York: Harper & Brothers, 1922), p. 311.

172 "I shall never get beyond . . . in America has faced": McFeely, *Frederick Douglass*, p. 385.

174 "Frederick Douglass": Robert Hayden, "Frederick Douglass," in Frederick Glaysher, ed., *Collected Poems: Robert Hayden* (New York: Liveright, 1997), p. 62.

Selected Sources

IN ADDITION TO THE SOURCES BELOW, I AM indebted to the Frederick Douglass Papers at the Library of Congress, a treasure trove of correspondence, legal and financial documents, scrapbooks, and more (www.loc.gov/collection/frederick-douglass-papers/about-this-collection).

*Suitable for readers 12 and up.

Blight, David W. *Frederick Douglass' Civil War: Keeping Faith in Jubilee*. Baton Rouge: Louisiana State University Press, revised edition, 1991.

*Bolden, Tonya. *Cause: Reconstruction America, 1863–1877*. New York: Alfred A. Knopf, 2005.

*——. *Emancipation Proclamation: Lincoln and the Dawn of Liberty*. New York: Abrams Books for Young Readers, 2013.

Chaffin, Tom. *Giant's Causeway: Frederick Douglass's Irish Odyssey and the Making of an American Visionary*. Charlottesville: University of Virginia Press, 2014, Kindle edition.

Douglass, Frederick. *Life and Times of Frederick Douglass*. Boston: De Wolfe & Fiske Co., 1892.

——. *My Bondage and My Freedom*. New York: Miller, Orton & Mulligan, 1855.

Foner, Philip S., and Yuval Taylor, eds. *Frederick Douglass: Selected Speeches and Writings*. Chicago: Lawrence Hill Books, 1999. Kindle edition.

Gates, Henry Louis Jr., ed. *Frederick Douglass: Autobiographies*. New York: The Library of America, 1994.

Lee, Maurice S., ed. *The Cambridge Companion to Frederick Douglass*. Cambridge, England: Cambridge University Press, 2009.

Levine, Robert S. *The Lives of Frederick Douglass*. Cambridge, Massachusetts: Harvard University Press, 2016. Kindle edition.

——. *Martin Delany, Frederick Douglass, and the Politics of Representative Identity*. Chapel Hill, NC: University of North Carolina Press, 2000, Kindle edition.

Luria, Sarah. *Capital Speculations: Writings and Building Washington, D.C.* Durham, New Hampshire: University of New Hampshire Press, paperback, 2005.

Martin, Waldo E. *The Mind of Frederick Douglass*. Chapel Hill, North Carolina: University of North Carolina Press, paperback, 1984.

McFeely, William S. *Frederick Douglass*. New York: W.W. Norton, paperback, 1995.

McKivigan, John R., ed. *The Frederick Douglass Papers, Series Three: Correspondence, Volume 1, 1842–1852*. New Haven: Yale University Press, 2009.

Muller, John. *Frederick Douglass in Washington, D.C.: The Lion of Anacostia*. Charleston, South Carolina: The History Press, 2012. Kindle edition.

O'Keefe, Rose. *Frederick & Anna Douglass in Rochester, New York: Their Home Was Open to All*. Charleston, South Carolina: The History Press, 2013 Kindle Edition.

SELECTED SOURCES

Stauffer, John. *The Black Hearts of Men: Radical Abolitionists and the Transformation of Race*. Cambridge, Massachusetts: Harvard University Press, 2002. Kindle edition.

———. *Giants: The Parallel Lives of Frederick Douglass and Abraham Lincoln*. New York: Twelve, 2008. Kindle edition.

Stauffer, John, Zoe Trodd, and Celeste-Marie Bernier. *Picturing Frederick Douglass: An Illustrated Biography of the Nineteenth Century's Most Photographed American*. New York: Liveright, 2015.

* Thompson, Julius E., James L. Conyers Jr., and Nancy J. Dawson, eds. *The Frederick Douglass Encyclopedia*. Santa Barbara, CA: Greenwood Press, 2010.

Acknowledgments

GREAT GRATITUDE TO THE GREAT ABRAMS TEAM: editor Howard Reeves, assistant editor Orlando Dos Reis, editorial assistant Masha Gunic, managing editors James Armstrong and Amy Vreeland, copyeditor Renée Cafiero, proofreaders Zachary Greenwald and Dru-Ann Chuckran; associate art director Pamela Notarantonio, designer Sara Corbett, and associate production director Alison Gervais.

For their prompt and generous response to my inquiries about images or other matters, I thank: African American history and culture specialist for the manuscript division Dr. Adrienne Cannon, and educational resource specialist Danna Bell, at the Library of Congress; specialist in early nineteenth-century photography Greg French; Harvard University professor of English and American literature, American studies, and African American studies John Stauffer; archivist and records manager at the New England Conservatory, Maryalice Perrin-Mohr; assistant registrar David Dziardziel and archivist Brendan Higgins at the Boston Conservatory; librarian Mark Procknik and curator Arthur Motta at the New Bedford Whaling

Museum; and curator of the Frederick Douglass National Historic Site, Kamal McClarin.

For reading and feedback on a near-final draft of the manuscript I thank the College of New Jersey associate professor of journalism and professional writing Kim Pearson. For helping me clear permissions, I thank my sister, Nelta. And for her steady, ongoing support I thank my agent, Jennifer Lyons.

Image Credits

Page iv: Profile *Portrait of Frederick Douglass*, c. 1858, by unidentified photographer, The Nelson-Atkins Museum of Art, Kansas City, Missouri. Gift of Hallmark Cards, Inc. 2005.27.42 © Nelson Gallery Foundation. Photo; Thomas Palmer. Page viii: *Frederick Douglass* c. 1841, by unidentified photographer, collection of Greg French. Page 2: Detail from *South-Eastern View of New Bedford, Mass.*, drawn by J. W. Barber, engraved by S. E. Brown, author's collection. Page 4: *William Lloyd Garrison*, by Southworth and Hawes, Private collector. Page 7: Detail from *Charles Lenox Remond*, by Samuel Broadbent, Boston Public Library. Page 14: *Captain Thomas Auld*, by unidentified photographer, Maryland State Archives. Page 17: *Frederick Douglass*, by unidentified photographer, Collection of the Onondaga Historical Association, Syracuse, NY. Page 19: Frontispiece and title page of *Narrative*, by unidentified engraver, Library of Congress. Pages 22–23: *The Anti-Slavery Society Convention, 1840*, by Benjamin Robert Haydon © National Portrait Gallery, London. Page 25: Detail from *Daniel O'Connell*, by Sir George Hayter © National Portrait Gallery, London. Pages 28–29: *View of Edinburgh from the Ramparts of the Castle, Looking East*, by David Roberts, National Galleries of Scotland. Page 36: *Frederick Douglass*, by unidentified photographer, National Portrait Gallery, Smithsonian Institution. Page 40: *23d Anti-Slavery Bazaar*, Library of Congress. Pages 42–43: Rochester, by G. G. Lange, published by Charles Magnus, author's collection. Page 45: *North Star*, Maryland State Archives. Page 46: Detail from *William Cooper Nell*, by unidentified engraver and photographer, Collection of the Massachusetts Historical Society. Page 52: *Frederick Douglass*, by Edward White Gallery, Chester County Historical Society, West Chester, PA. Page 58: Detail from *William Howard Day*, Wilson Library, University of North Carolina at Chapel Hill. Page 59: Detail from *Portrait of John Jones*, by Aaron E. Darling, Chicago History Museum, CHi-62629. Page 64: Detail from *Gerrit Smith*, by unidentified photographer, Boston Public Library. Page 65: *North Star*, from the collection of the Local History & Genealogy Division, Rochester (NY) Public Library. Page 67: *Frederick Douglass*, 1847/52, by Samuel J. Miller, Art Institute of Chicago. Page

IMAGE CREDITS

71: *Frederick Douglass' Paper*, from the collection of the Local History and Genealogy Division, Rochester, NY, Public Library. Pages 82, 83: Detail from *Henry Highland Garnet*, by Rockwood & Co., and *Martin Robison Delany*, by unidentified photographer, Collection of Greg French. Page 84: Detail from *John Brown* by unidentified photographer, the Boston Athenaeum. Page 90: *Douglass' Monthly*, special collections, Lavery Library. St. John Fisher College, Rochester, NY. Page 92: *Frederick Douglass*, by Edwin Burke Ives and Reuben L. Andrews, photograph courtesy of Hillsdale College. Pages 100–101: *The Effects of the Proclamation*, author's collection. Page 102: *Men of Color! To Arms!*, Library Company of Philadelphia. Pages 104, 107, 108–109: *Storming Fort Wagner*, published by Kurz & Allison, detail from *Abraham Lincoln, Sunday, November 8, 1863*, by Alexander Gardner, and The Fall of Richmond, published by Currier & Ives, Library of Congress. Page 110: *Frederick Douglass*, by Henry P. Rundel and Charles Warren Woodward, Beinecke Rare Book and Manuscript Library/Yale University. Pages 115, 123, 126: Untitled ambrotype, by unidentified photographer; Representative Women, by L. Schamer, published by L. Prang & Co.; *Frederick Douglass*, by unidentified photographer, Library of Congress. Pages 128–129: *The Smithsonian Institution Building from Pennsylvania Ave., 1874*, by William Henry Holmes, Smithsonian Institution Archives Image #MAH-48646. Page 131: *New National Era*, Library of Congress. Page 133, images 1, 2, 3, and 4 and page 135: Courtesy of the National Park Service, Frederick Douglass National Historic Site, Washington, D.C.; *Charles R. Douglass* (FRDO 3908), Frederick Douglass Jr. (FRDO4954), *Lewis and Amelia Douglass* (FRDO 4552), *Rosetta D. Sprague* (FRDO 4812), and *Frederick Douglass in Front of His A Street NE Home* (FRDO 11001). Page 137: *The Department of Justice (Freedman's Bank Building)*, by unidentified photographer, Library of Congress. Page 141: *Ohio—The Republican National Convention at Cincinnati*, Susan H. Douglas Political Americana Collection—#2214 Rare and Manuscript Collections, Cornell University Library, Cornell University. Page 143: *The First Colored Senator and Representatives*, published by Currier & Ives, Library of Congress. Pages 146, 148, 151, 153: Courtesy of the National Park Service; Frederick Douglass National Historic Site, Washington, D.C.; *Snow at Cedar Hill in 1887* (FRDO2816); *Anna M. Douglass* (FDRO246); *Helen Pitts Douglass* (FRDO318); *Frederick Douglass at His Desk in Haiti*, by W. Watson (FDRO 3899). Page 161: Page one of letter, Library of Congress. Page 163: *Formal portrait of Frederick Douglass and His Grandson Joseph*, Notman Photographic Co., Boston, Schlesinger Library, Radcliffe Institute, Harvard University. Page 165: *Ida B. Wells*, National Portrait Gallery, Smithsonian Institution. Page 166: Courtesy of the National Park Service, Frederick Douglass National Historic Site, Washington, D.C., *Frederick Douglass in His Study at Cedar Hill* (FRDO 3886). Page 168: *Frederick Douglass*, by Phineas C. Headley Jr. and James E. Reed, Courtesy of the New Bedford Whaling Museum. Page 171, images 1, 2, and 3: Courtesy of the National Park Service, Frederick Douglass National Historic Site, Washington, D.C.: inkstand, top hat, and stereoscope. Page 173: *Frederick Douglass* by unidentified photographer, courtesy of the Moorland-Spingarn Research Center, Howard University Archives, Howard University, Washington, D.C.

Index

Note: Page numbers in *italic* refer to illustrations.

INDEX